Gamification for Employee Engagement

Strategize, design, and implement gamification to successfully engage your employees

Akila Narayanan

Gamification for Employee Engagement

First published: December 2014

Production Reference: 1241214

Published by Impackt Publishing Ltd.
Livery Place
35 Livery Street
Birmingham B3 2PB, UK.

ISBN 978-1-78300-134-7

www.Impacktpub.com

Credits

Author

Akila Narayanan

Reviewers

Sanjay Abraham

Mohit Garg

Commissioning Editor

Richard Gall

Content Development Editor

Amey Varangaonkar

Copy Editors

Ankur Ghiye

Rohith Rajan

Project Coordinator

Priyanka Goel

Proofreaders

Simran Bhogal

Maria Gould

Ameesha Green

Paul Hindle

Production Coordinator

Melwyn D'sa

Cover Work

Simon Cardew

About the Author

 **Akila Narayanan** has over a decade of experience in the IT industry and is currently working as a project manager with one of the global IT leaders. She is a social business enthusiast and evangelist with vast experience managing complex and strategic projects for insurance customers. She specializes in enabling social business and gamification for insurance customers, has published thought papers and created customer mindshare. She is an avid blogger in her organizational community and her areas of interest include project management, people/ human resource management, behavioral analysis, motivation, process and quality, knowledge management, social business, gamification, and innovation. She is also interested in convergence of social, mobile, cloud, and analytics technologies. She has a strong passion for enabling people, a keen observer and an empathic thinker. She holds a Bachelor's degree in engineering from University of Madras and is PMP, AINS certified. She has completed the online gamification course offered by `coursera.org`.

Akila Narayanan is based out of Chennai, India. She can be reached at `https://www.linkedin.com/pub/akila-narayanan/46/27b/403`.

Acknowledgments

Thanks to one and all at Impackt Publishing for having given me this maiden opportunity. The entire crew behind the scenes deserves fullest credits for their fantastic work and support.

Thanks to my parents Sumathi and Narayanan, for being my life support system. Whatever I am today, I owe it all to you.

Thanks to my role model and friend Anuradha Sundararajan, for being an eternal source of inspiration. You made all the difference in my life.

Thanks to my best friend Deepa Manjari Sampathrao, for being the best. I know you will stand by me, no matter what.

Thanks to my batch mates Kumaravel Manickam Kandan and Raam Vaidyanathan, for being there, always. I cherish your friendship a lot.

Thanks to Raveendran N in whose small firm I learnt to crawl as a professional, and Mohan Subramanian for referring me to a corporate organization.

Thanks to the thought leaders Ashok Kumar Jothimani, Sukumar Rajagopal, and Shyam Sundar Nagarajan, who have shaped, inspired, and influenced me respectively in the professional arena.

Thanks to Ashok, you led by example demonstrating the value of employee engagement. I developed a lot of professional traits by observing you in close quarters. In fact, you introduced me to blogging and that has done a world of good for me.

Thanks to Sukumar, you inspired me through illuminating blog posts, encouraged me with your thoughtful comments, nudged me the most to write a book, especially pointed out the value of non-fiction writing to me.

Thanks to Shyam, you introduced me to Whitepapers, imparted knowledge on the subject of gamification, made me feel valued for my contributions at the workplace, and rekindled the passion and much more.

Thanks to Kevin Werbach whose brilliant online course I attended on gamification through https://www.coursera.org/. I recommend the course to each one of you interested in the subject.

Thanks to my blogging gurus Meenakshisankar M and Anbu Muppidathi and the entire blogging community of my current organization for their constant encouragement and support.

Thanks to my favorite boss Lakshmi Narasimhan Srinivasan and to all the other esteemed bosses and leads from whom I have learned the nuances of employee engagement. And thanks to all those friends, colleagues, relatives, and well-wishers whom I couldn't single out here but have helped me in one way or the other in my journey of life.

Thanks a bunch to God for bringing all these wonderful people into my lives. Special thanks to all those wonderful readers, who would be buying (hopefully) or who would happen to read this book.

About the Reviewers

Sanjay Abraham is a social business, gamification, analytics and mobility consultant. He has 15 years of experience into software consulting, understanding business needs and positioning the right software solutions for enterprises. His personal area of passion is to help enterprises have the right digital strategy through Social, Mobile, Analytics and Cloud (SMAC). As an evangelist and consultant into social business, gamification, analytics and mobile, he helps enterprises redefine the way business is done.

He has a flair for writing on technology and business topics too and is a regular blogger at Innovation, Insights or WIRED, Business2Community, Yahoo, SAP, IBM, and Jive communities. He is also featured as a Social Business thought leader by Jive in January 2014.

Sanjay staunchly believes, digital transformation could radically change the way business is done. Presently, enterprises get just 45 percent value from their existing technology systems. As embracing digital transformation could often be a daunting task for enterprises, his initiative called Enterprise CLINIC, which he passionately drives, is to help organizations visualize and explore new technologies and evaluate products and platform.

He is experienced into Enterprise Collaboration, Social Business, Enterprise Social network (ESN), Enterprise Innovation Management (EIM), Social Onboarding and Learning, Social Project Management, Communities Management, Gamification, Enterprise Mobility- Mobile Device and Content Management, BYOD, Big Data Analytics and Data Visualization, Enterprise File Sync and Sharing (EFSS), content collaboration and Enterprise Identity and Access Management (EIAM).

Presently, he works as Director- Consulting with CTPRD and drives new technology initiatives in the social, analytics, and mobility space for verticals such BFSI, Government, ITeS, Insurance, Education, Retail and so on.

Prior to this, his assignments were with IT giants such as Tech Mahindra as DGM and Avaya GCL as Head of Business Applications.

He holds a Bachelor's degree in engineering (Computer Science) and PG diploma in Business Management both from Barkatullah University, Bhopal, India.

Mohit Garg is the co-founder of a fast-growing technology company, MindTickle and an avid gamification evangelist and blogger. He has co-authored IEEE publication titled *Application of Online Gamification to New Hire Onboarding* (ISBN: 978-1-4673-5729-6).

MindTickle is a social and gamified platform for next generation online learning. MindTickle was awarded the #1 platform globally at the Gamification Summit, San Francisco for the *Best use of engagement techniques in HR* and *Cool Vendor* by Gartner. MindTickle serves over 65,000 corporate learners today from several Fortune 500 and leading organizations across the globe.

Mohit has a diverse work experience spanning across 16 years and four continents. Prior to cofounding MindTickle, he was the Director in PwC's management consulting practice at New York, and has been a senior member of product teams in the Silicon Valley. He was awarded as Entrepreneur of the Year by Startup Leadership Program (SLP) in 2012. Mohit holds an MBA degree from the Indian School of Business and MSEE from Stanford University.

Mohit lives at Mountain View, California and enjoys running, snowboarding, and spending time with his one-year-old son.

Contents

Chapter 2: Gamification in Action   29

Chapter 3: Enterprise Gamification – Strategize   51

Chapter 6: Sustaining Outcomes and the Road Ahead   117

Preface

There are certain buzzwords that are more intriguing than the rest. Gamification is one such buzzword. This is not surprising as the origins are traced back to the world of games. It is quite amusing that the term is ambiguous for both novices and intellects. While novices misconstrue gamification as playing games, intellects brush it off as yet another variation of a loyalty or rewards program. But what is it, actually?

Of course there is some connection to games or a loyalty program.

Don't we get completely engrossed while playing games?

Don't we get motivated to undertake an activity to win incentives?

Gamification borrows these best practices and applies them in a non-game context to influence humans to behave in certain ways. But there's a lot more to it. Instead of focusing too much on confining the boundaries of gamification, we should approach it as a problem solving or motivational technique to accomplish desired outcomes. Anything that serves the purpose of influencing the user to behave in a desired manner joins the gamification club.

Exaggerating that thought a little further, I view gamification as a friend in need. It can be treated as a virtual companion, a coach, or a motivator that has a fair understanding about the operating context and the user. It helps the user overcome fatigue or anxiety and keeps the user engaged in pursuing activities that are for the common good. This presents significant opportunities for business enterprises to reinvent their engagement strategies when it concerns their employees, partners, or customers.

While there is a plethora of possibilities for enterprises, in this book we will be deliberating on driving employee engagement using gamification. As a gamification enthusiast, my intention is to take you through a journey where you can appreciate the applicability of gamification to solve specific problems that are faced by employers in workplace concerning employee engagement.

The concepts, methodologies, processes, and the techniques referred to in this book might not be entirely new. You will instead find an actionable approach to strategize, design, and implement an enterprise gamification system deploying these processes or techniques in the appropriate fashion. This book is written keeping in mind the present trends in the workplace that concern disengagement, specifically addressing the expectations of the millennial or new age workforce. I can certainly promise to serve you an assortment of ideas sprinkled with interesting correlations. Indeed, this book will ignite your minds to harness the power of gamification.

What this book covers

Chapter 1, Employee Engagement and Gamification, will enable you to understand the changing expectations of the new age workforce and the causes behind employee disengagement in the workplace. We will further learn how gamification can act as a catalyst in driving engagement.

Chapter 2, Gamification in Action, will show you how to put gamification into action within varied business processes and achieve improved employee productivity, reduced employee turnover, improved sales performance, enhanced collaboration, and in turn improve quality of service to customers.

Chapter 3, Enterprise Gamification – Strategize, will teach you to devise a strategy aligning gamification with business objectives. It will enable you to understand the target audience behavior in order to deliver an engaging experience based on the user's needs and expectations.

Chapter 4, Enterprise Gamification – Design, will help you learn how to apply design thinking to gamification. You will learn the design thinking process of researching, ideating, prototyping, testing, and iterating over loops to gather end user feedback early in the life cycle.

Chapter 5, Enterprise Gamification – Implementation, will show you how to go about the implementation journey. We will study how to start small with a pilot implementation and ascertain the outcome from the pilot findings before eventually scaling to a full-blown implementation.

Chapter 6, Sustaining Outcomes and the Road Ahead, will show you how to sustain the outcomes and highlight on few adoption strategies. In this chapter, I have captured my viewpoint on what's in store with regards to the future of gamification in both the short and long term.

Who this book is for

This book is primarily targeted at those who are looking to engage a certain section of employees within an enterprise. Having said that, this book can be read by all professionals representing both the employer and the employee community as everyone has a part to play in creating a collaborative culture and sustaining engagement in the workplace. The topic applies commonly to all workforces irrespective of the industry they represent or the roles they play. The book has more references to the IT profession in the practical illustrations, as the author belongs to that breed. Preliminary knowledge on gamification would certainly help, but this is not a prerequisite as the book is written in a very simple fashion with practical illustrations explaining the fundamentals before diving deep.

Conventions

In this book, you will find a number of styles of text that distinguish between different kinds of information. Here are some examples of these styles, and an explanation of their meaning.

New terms and important words are shown in bold.

Make a note
Warnings or important notes appear in a box like this.

Reader feedback

Feedback from our readers is always welcome. Let us know what you think about this book—what you liked or may have disliked. Reader feedback is important for us to develop titles that you really get the most out of.

To send us general feedback, simply send an e-mail to feedback@impacktpub.com, and mention the book title via the subject of your message.

If there is a book that you need and would like to see us publish, please send us a note via the **Submit Idea** form on https://www.impacktpub.com/#!/bookidea.

Piracy

Piracy of copyright material on the Internet is an ongoing problem across all media. At Packt, we take the protection of our copyright and licenses very seriously. If you come across any illegal copies of our works, in any form, on the Internet, please provide us with the location address or website name immediately so that we can pursue a remedy.

Please contact us at copyright@impacktpub.com with a link to the suspected pirated material.

We appreciate your help in protecting our authors, and our ability to bring you valuable content.

> 1

Employee Engagement and Gamification

It is a well-established fact that an engaged workforce delivers strong business outcomes. Gauging **employee engagement** levels through research findings or surveys clearly indicates that most organizations struggle to keep their workforce engaged. Lately, **gamification** has manifested success in influencing a person's behavior towards producing the desired outcome. Why are we associating employee engagement and gamification? In this book, we set out on a journey that will hopefully help us unravel this mystery.

In this chapter, we will cover:

- ➤ What constitutes employee engagement
- ➤ What is enterprise gamification
- ➤ How gamification acts as a catalyst to drive employee engagement
- ➤ The new age workforce

We now live in an era where globalization trends, economic shifts, societal reforms, and technological advents have converged to redefine both our personal and professional landscape. There are a large number of disruptive forces like IT consumerization, social collaboration, and virtualization that have stormed into the business world, propelling organizations to rethink their corporate strategies. One significant climate change is the surge of **millennials,** more commonly known as **Gen Y**, who are estimated to make up nearly half of the workforce by 2020 as predicted by the U.S. Bureau of Labor Statistics.

Of late, business organizations face major challenges in attracting, nurturing, and retaining the right mix of talent. At large, **Baby Boomers** or **Gen X** occupying the executive managerial positions at these organizations fail to understand the changing expectations of the millennial workforce, who not only comprise of the newer employee base, but also largely constitute the newer customer base.

Enterprises need to have a comprehensive understanding of the multi-generation employees and their expectations, so that the employee engagement strategies can be tailored according to their target audience.

Understanding the employee needs

Most enterprises have largely followed a hierarchical organizational structure backed by procedural norms, stringent processes, and standard work profiles that has worked relatively well with the generations of the past.

Baby Boomers

In relation to employee expectations, Baby Boomers lay importance to job security and financial stability, and are in turn willing to invest in long working hours with the utmost commitment and loyalty. They are extremely perseverant to work their way up to the top of the ladder gradually. As long as their basic financial needs are met, monotonous work doesn't seem to hamper their engagement levels.

Gen X

Though Gen X enrolls in the hierarchical culture, they expect more flexibility at their workplace, both in terms of work hours and their job profiles. They prefer meritocracy over experience to climb up the ladder. They are willing to accommodate, but engagement levels dip and loyalty does take a backseat if the job profile gets too repetitive. As long as the organizations rotate them to meaningful roles with adequate responsibilities and cater to their long-term aspirations, they will continue to serve to the best of their abilities.

Gen Y/Millennials

Workplace demographics have undergone a sea of change in the recent past with the entry of tech-savvy and hyper-active millennials. Being brought up in a fast-paced and digitally-connected culture, they have unique expectations from their employers. It is imperative for organizations to clearly understand the expectations of their younger workforce to better drive and sustain their engagement.

The following are some key expectations that employers should pay heed to:

> **Defy hierarchy**: Millennials prefer a flat hierarchy over the traditional pyramid structure. Thanks to Internet technologies, they are supremely smart and well-exposed and don't subscribe to authoritative doctrines driven by sheer experience and positions. They have entrepreneurial spirits, and they don't give substantial weightage to formal education degrees as compared to on-the-job skills and innovation. As much as they respect experience, they believe in talent-driven and swift growth. They get to choose their jobs, employers, and bosses rather than the other way round.

> **Collaborative culture**: Having been immersed in the virtual world of social media, millennials love to work as a team and enroll in open, transparent, participative, and collaborative cultures. They base most of their decisions on the recommendations from their peers, and they would like to extend that same culture at their workplace by collaborating and co-ideating with their colleagues.

> **Empowerment and trust**: Millennials develop a sense of belongingness towards their organization if they are allowed to participate in important discussions, express their views freely, and showcase their creative abilities to make an impact in the accomplishment of the end objectives. Despite the challenges involved in a task, if they are empowered and entrusted, they deliver it with panache. They hate to be micro-managed as they view it as distrust. As against common perceptions, it is not the paycheck that matters to them most. If they love the job on hand and are allowed to operate freely with adequate autonomy, encouragement, and support from the management, they will be more engaged and surpass excellence more often.

> **Instant feedback**: Rapid accessibility is of key priority to millennials, both in terms of seeking information and feedback. They expect their employers and supervisors to be responsive to their needs and demands. They can be termed as the fast-food generation who instantly expect a response, instantly warrant feedback, instantly anticipate recognition and growth, instantly get motivated, instantly get disengaged, and instantly look out for alternatives if the engagement levels are not sustained.

> **Flexible environment**: Millennials expect flexibility with respect to many aspects at the workplace. They prefer the flexibility to work from anywhere, anytime rather than being confined to cubicles with rigid timings. They favor a lenient dress code policy and prefer casual over formal attire. They prefer to attend training programs aligned to their career aspirations and contribute to organizational initiatives in line with their personal interests.

> **Sense of purpose**: Millennials always respect and contribute to initiatives that have a sense of purpose and demonstrate goodwill in supporting the community. They have a deeper sense of responsibility as a citizen and stand by those brands and business organizations that establish a corporate social responsibility towards their community. If they can identify the goals of the organization, they will give it their all.

The employee engagement rules of the past might no longer be relevant to a new age workforce; its time to reinvent.

A classic case of employee engagement

Before developing strategies to engage employees within an organization, it is important to understand what employee engagement actually is.

A story scenario

Sam works as a project lead in an IT company. He has a team of 10 members under him and they have been working on a critical customer-facing project with stiff deadlines. After 8 months of slogging, the team has successfully delivered the code and the User Acceptance Testing has been signed-off by the customer. Tim, Rina, and Kevin are the three senior developers who have invested extra efforts and have been waiting for an opportunity to avail vacation. Sam approves their vacation and they are all set to leave to their respective hometowns the next morning.

Sam receives a call that evening from a customer that a certain bug has been uncovered before the production move, and they urgently need someone to support the fix.

Sam calls up the three team members individually and asks them whether they can support the emergency situation.

Tim retaliates, "Sam, could you check this with Rina? She just got promoted and ideally she should own this up."

Rina reacts, "Sam, I would love to take this up because this project got me recognition. But I am afraid I can't cancel this personal vacation. Can you make an alternate arrangement? I can definitely support the team over call or e-mail."

Kevin responds, "Sam, our months of hard work might go to waste if this bug turns up in production and our organization's reputation might be at stake considering the criticality of the project. Let me report to the office tomorrow postponing the vacation."

Inference

In the case presented earlier, Tim seems demotivated because of a denied personal recognition and chooses to pass the buck. Rina, though motivated by her recent elevation, is looking for alternate options to somehow manage the situation rather than owning it up. Whereas Kevin seems to be the engaged employee, who goes beyond his call of duty and demonstrates a sense of ownership and accountability.

Research studies prove that engaged employees establish a strong emotional connect with the organization or job and are willing to invest discretionary efforts. Employee engagement can be defined as the degree to which an employee is bonded towards his organization or job.

The following are some of the key characteristics that define an engaged employee:

- ➤ They understand the holistic picture and strategic objectives of the organization.
- ➤ They are self-driven, staying focused in accomplishing the end objectives.
- ➤ They are passionate about their work.
- ➤ They place their job priority above personal priorities.
- ➤ They are accountable, take complete ownership, and travel the extra mile.
- ➤ They are persistent and not bogged down by temporary setbacks.
- ➤ They are participative in team discussions and provide suggestions for improvement.
- ➤ They are optimistic and work effectively in a team setup by collaborating with others.
- ➤ They solicit constructive feedback and constantly upgrade their skills.
- ➤ They have a sense of belongingness and take pride in associating themselves with the organization.

An engaged employee is in a *self-actualized state of being*, peaking the pyramid of motivation as proposed by Maslow.

> **Make a note**
>
> Read more on Maslow's hierarchy of needs at `http://en.wikipedia.org/wiki/Maslow's_hierarchy_of_needs`.

Employee engagement quotient and the 5 Whys

Every organization devises their own means of gauging their employee engagement levels, and typically, a survey is launched for the employees to gather their feedback.

Employee engagement survey

Given below is a simple employee engagement survey, a fairly quick means of determining the levels of engagement.

Never (Score: 0 points); Sometimes yes (Score: 1 point); Always (Score: 2 points)

Sr. No.	Question	Never	Sometimes yes	Always
1.	Do I feel passionate about my job?			
2.	Do I have a sense of belongingness towards my organization?			
3.	Do I feel empowered to voice my opinions freely?			
4.	Do I feel that my ideas are invited and implemented?			
5.	Am I valued and recognized for my contributions?			
6.	Do I feel challenged and inspired to meet my goals?			
7.	Do I receive constant support and encouragement from my supervisor(s)?			
8.	Do we collaborate and work well as a team in the peer group?			
9.	Am I given the opportunity that aligns with my career aspirations?			

Sr. No.	Question	Never	Sometimes yes	Always
10.	Do I feel accountable for my errors and omissions?			
11.	Would I work with the organization on long-term basis?			
12.	Would I refer my friends to join this organization?			

> ➤ A score of (0 – 8) points indicates that your employees are *highly disengaged.*
> ➤ A score of (9 – 16) points indicates that your employees are *somewhat engaged.*
> ➤ A score of (17 – 24) points indicates that your employees are *highly engaged.*

Though the employee identity can be anonymous, it helps to collect some generic profile information on the age, gender, department, number of years of service with the company, and supervisor information to drill down the data further and understand where to lay focus. If the employee engagement quotient, that is, the number of employees highly engaged in proportion to overall employee headcount, is low, enterprises need to follow up with a detailed root cause analysis to assess the drivers of disengagement and revisit their systems, processes, and policies in place.

Common causes of disengagement

A recent survey from **Gallup Inc.**, a research-based global performance-management consulting company, indicates that only 30% of American employees are engaged at the workplace. That is quite an alarming trend and needs serious retrospection as to what leads to disengagement.

Understanding the root cause behind employee disengagement is a critical step, and one useful technique in digging deep is the 5 Why Analysis.

A story scenario

Richard was a star performer in ABC team, and his performance has deteriorated over the last few months. Asking a series of Whys might lead us to the root cause:

1. Why? – He doesn't report to work regularly (the first why).
2. Why? – He is not motivated to work in ABC team (the second why).
3. Why? – The tasks he performs in ABC team don't interest him (the third why).
4. Why? – The tasks assigned to him are monotonous in nature (the fourth why).
5. Why? – The job profile mismatches with his skill levels and aspirations (fifth why and the root cause).

The solution

Match Richard's job profile with his skill levels and aspirations. Replace him with a junior level resource to perform his current tasks and offer challenging assignments to Richard.

In this scenario, by using the 5 Whys technique, we have figured out the root cause behind the disengagement and came up with a possible solution.

An employee always forms part of an organizational ecosystem where they are surrounded by three core entities within the organization. When they are *misaligned* with the key attributes or the stakeholders involving these entities, it might escalate to disengagement.

Entity	Key Attributes	Stakeholders
Organization	Vision, Culture, Leadership, Systems, Processes, Policies	Executive Leadership, Senior Management
Current Department	Mentoring, Support, Relationship, Job Profile, Role	Supervisor, Peers, Subordinates
Support Functions	Talent and Performance Management, Compensation and Benefits, Training	Co-workers from other departments (HR, Finance, Training Executives)

The common causes of disengagement include:

> Lack of vision and thinking in leadership

> Lack of purpose, goals, and expectations

> Lack of training and support

> Lack of open and transparent culture

> Strained relationship with supervisor or peers

> Job profile and skill level mismatch

> Mundane tasks at work

> Outdated systems and processes

> Lack of job stability

> Lack of rewards and recognition

> Poor performance management

> Lack of periodic and constructive feedback

The right pay for the right job has become more of a prerequisite for an employee when choosing a job. While compensation can satisfy employees to a certain extent, they don't have a direct influence or impact on the engagement levels. In some cases, *disengagement can be completely attributed to the idiosyncrasies* of the individuals, for example, some employees might have the tendency to procrastinate, and some might inherently lack team spirit.

Organizations need to carry out a formal evaluation of their employee engagement levels, identify the prominent causes towards disengagement, and implement strategies to avert them in order to retain and extract the optimal value out of their talent mix.

Driving engagement the SMART way

Before moving on to attaining the highest degree of engagement, we have to get the nitty-gritties right in driving engagement at a fundamental level. There are five factors that prescribe an employee's expectations at the workplace. Those termed as the **SMART** factors include **Satisfaction**, **Motivation**, **Advancement**, **Recognition**, and **Trust**.

Satisfaction

A satisfied employee need not be an engaged employee, but an engaged employee is almost always a satisfied employee. At the outset, job satisfaction indicates the degree to which an employee is content with their job, whereas engagement bespeaks the degree to which an employee goes beyond the call of duty. 75 – 80% of employees can be satisfied if they are assured of the following factors:

➤ Job security

➤ Financial stability

➤ Compensation

➤ Benefits

➤ Flexibility at the workplace

While satisfaction can't directly contribute to engagement, it can certainly disturb the engagement level if not taken care of.

Motivation

A satisfied employee need not be a motivated employee and a motivated employee need not be an engaged employee, whereas an engaged employee is almost always *a satisfied-cum-motivated employee*. **Motivation** refers to the psychological drive that reinforces one's action towards accomplishing a task or goal. It clearly indicates why an employee behaves in a certain fashion.

When comprehending motivation, it is essential to understand the two major types of motivation, namely **extrinsic** and **intrinsic** motivation.

Extrinsic motivation

Extrinsic motivation refers to the *motivation that is attained by an external push or outcomes.*

For example, if you accomplish task X, then we offer you Y as outcome. Y could constitute money, rewards, and status, or it could even be a penalty. Here, the motivation to perform or the anxiety to perform is driven by external forces and the sustenance is guaranteed as long as the outcome is clearly articulated and awarded on time.

Intrinsic motivation

Intrinsic motivation refers to the motivation that is attained by an internal push, only as much as the task interests oneself. Here, the motivation to perform comes from within, as the employee derives some sense of pleasure in undertaking the task and thereby longer sustenance is guaranteed.

An employee would implicitly tell themselves that if they accomplish task X, then they would derive Y as outcome. Y could constitute happiness, a sense of accomplishment, skill upgrade, or it could even be fear of losing self-respect. You might agree that many of us have certain expectations from ourselves and feel miserable not when we lose, but when we fail to invest efforts or perform to the best of our abilities.

On the contrary to extrinsic motivation where Y is more tangible, here, Y is more intangible, and we value it mostly for ourselves.

A story scenario

There is a kid in my avenue that cries non-stop and creates a huge scene on Monday mornings to not go to school. Even as grown-up adults, we hate Monday mornings, don't we?

The parents then make it a habit to buy the kid a chocolate if he/she attends school regularly on Mondays. The kid infers that if he/she resists going to school, the parents will buy a chocolate. The kid starts crying on Tuesday mornings too and the parents are forced to buy chocolates on Tuesdays too. The kid continues the trend for all the weekdays and the parents struggle in dealing with the kid's stubbornness and are clueless what to do next.

What would be your suggestion to the kid's parents? Do you think they had the right strategy in the first place to deal with the problem? Given their current strategy, do you think they should entertain the kid's request in the longer run? Mind you, this might finally land the kid at a dentist's clinic for treating a tooth cavity.

Inference

Many times, employers think that extrinsic motivation works best, but tend to overlook the fact that it purely depends on how the employees perceive it, and their strategies could completely backfire, leaving the sustenance at bay. We need a strategy that works beyond carrots and sticks at the workplace to attain the desired levels of engagement.

Advancement

Advancement refers to the growth in one's career in terms of designation or position, usually in relation to their good performance. This can also involve advancement in terms of gaining knowledge, skills, and maturity to move to the next level or undertake challenging assignments. Millennials usually expect quality time from their supervisors to mentor and guide them towards career progression in alignment with their aspirations. Advancement again can be intrinsic in the manner in which an employee feels that they have come a long way being part of the continuous journey of learning.

Recognition

Recognition is commonly associated with rewards given as a token of appreciation for accomplishing excellence. It symbolizes acknowledgement of one's good work. From tangibles to virtual awards, recognition can reassure an employee of their value to the organization. Employers fail to realize that recognition need not always translate to something materialistic. What is of utmost importance with respect to recognition is timeliness and genuineness. A timely *Thank you* e-mail, pat on the back (literally), even a smile or a nod from a senior executive can be associated with recognition as it just represents that we are being valued and respected in the place where we belong. Many times, employees value recognition from their teams and peers as much as they value recognition when it flows top-down. An ambience needs to be created at the workplace, where each of us within a group values and recognizes each other's contribution. The ultimate means of recognition comes from respect and repute that an employee earns at the workplace.

Trust

First of all, an employee needs to develop a sense of trust in the organization's purpose of existence and directions from the executive leadership team. *Much of the disengagement surfaces when leaders fail to communicate a clear vision.* Secondly, how often do we hear the phrase, *Employees don't leave an organization but leave their supervisor?* However much an organization invests to build policies of faith and trust, there is a larger *onus* on the middle managers and supervisors to ensure that it is established on the ground with their subordinates in the truest sense. The highest point of trust is accomplished when an employee is able to expose their vulnerabilities to the supervisor, seek help, and gain wisdom. When things don't work the way they are planned, supervisors should lend the adequate support rather than blaming it squarely on the subordinates. *If the seed of transparency is deep-rooted on the soil of trust, loyalty can be harvested.* A simple rule to remember is, *trust is mutual.*

These SMART factors are more like prerequisites to drive engagement. The organization should strive to build a culture and environment where employees are satisfied with their basic needs, motivated to perform to the best of their abilities, feel assured of progressions, receive acknowledgement of their value, and feel part of a trusted group in order to drive deeper levels of engagement.

Now that we have the prerequisites lined up, it is time to dive deeper into levels of engagement.

A story scenario

Steve is the Regional Head who oversees the team of sales and marketing executives. While there is no dearth of talent in the individuals, Steve observes the following issues while carrying out a performance review for his region:

> ➤ The sales executives miss out on responding to customer e-mails promptly, which results in customer complaints.

> ➤ The sales executives often take vacation without prior intimation.

> ➤ The marketing executives don't pass on clear information about the prospects.

> ➤ The marketing executives don't keep the brochure updated in the sales repository.

> ➤ The marketing executives and sales executives don't collaborate well with each other.

> ➤ The sales and marketing teams are always at loggerheads, blaming each other in the case of missed targets.

> ➤ The region might miss accomplishing the targets as a team if the trend continues.

Steve convenes a meeting with his team and informs that there is a new announcement from his global head that the team that performs exceedingly well at regional levels will qualify for a big honor from the CEO of the firm. He points out the misalignment between the sales and marketing teams, and expresses concern. But he also assures that if both the parties start collaborating from then on, they could make it to the top of the charts.

Steve's team expresses certain concerns as to why they are unable to collaborate effectively and also assure him that they will make the necessary reforms at their end.

Steve comes up with a few initiatives to address the concerns and implements them promptly:

> ➤ He tracks and publishes the top salesman of the month, who got good feedback from the customers.

> ➤ He formalizes leave or vacation tracking in the system and shares the report with the team, honoring the consistently punctual employees with badges.

> ➤ He facilitates a channel for the sales and marketing executives to easily collaborate with each other and share knowledge and recognizes the valuable contributors.

> ➤ He provides access to both sales and marketing teams to a single integrated CRM system to maintain prospect and customer contacts and awards points for providing additional insights about the contacts that can translate to sales conversions.

Steve observes a significant change in the employees' behavior and his team does emerge as the top region of the year, meeting the revenue targets.

Inference

Whenever a group of individuals are entrusted with a task with clearly defined objectives and expectations, challenged to march towards a mission or a quest, establish prompt feedback loops, enable a platform for sharing knowledge, and collaborating and valued for their contributions, it brings the best out of them in the capacity of individuals and as a team. In a nutshell, the routine chores when gamified can seed deeper levels of engagement.

Defining enterprise gamification

Before delving into enterprise gamification, does "business enterprise" and "game" together sound like an oxymoron? You would be surprised to notice certain similarities between these two non-related terms.

A game can be thought to have certain attributes:

> - **Goal**: A player sets their eye on a target to achieve.
> - **Rules**: Structure and *How-To's* of a game.
> - **Player(s)**: One/many who participates.
> - **Outcome**: Declared a winner if the goals are met, lose otherwise.
> - **Feedback**: Player is kept updated of the progress.

If you observe closely, business enterprises also have relevance to the following attributes:

> - **Goal**: A business enterprise has strategic objectives to accomplish.
> - **Rules**: Structure and policies that govern the organization.
> - **Players**: Employees who work for the organization.
> - **Outcome**: Declared a success if the objectives are met, fail otherwise.
> - **Feedback**: Applicable both at an employee and organizational level to gauge their progress.

While a game is played mainly as a pastime fun activity, gamification doesn't exactly signify playing games. It refers to the application of game design thinking in non-game contexts to engage users. In other words, we incite the user by turning a purposeful activity into an engaging one by delivering a game-like experience.

Before proceeding further, it is important to understand the distinction between these terminologies below:

> ➤ **Fun game**: An actual game played for the purpose of pure fun or entertainment.

> ➤ **Serious game**: An actual game played for a meaningful purpose apart from pure fun or entertainment.

> ➤ **Gamification**: A non-game context is transformed into game-like experience leveraging attributes derived from game psychology.

Gaming is often associated with the spirit of one party winning and the other party losing. On the contrary, in the context of an enterprise, gamification can act as a *catalyst* that improves employee engagement, thereby resulting in a *win-win* situation for both employer and employee. A good gamification platform can help employers understand and influence the behavior of their employees to work towards accomplishing the desired outcome. In order to envision and design such a platform, it requires a comprehensive understanding of game thinking so that it can be leveraged to influence the behavior of an employee.

Have you ever felt like being completely immersed in an activity when you don't hear the loud utterances from your mom or spouse, the ringtone of the phone, the whir of a fan or air conditioner, or the noise of a ticking clock? This is what is termed as the optimal point of engagement called **flow zone,** as proposed by Mihaly Csikszentmihalyi.

Make a note

Read more about the concept of flow (psychology) at `http://en.wikipedia.org/wiki/Flow`.

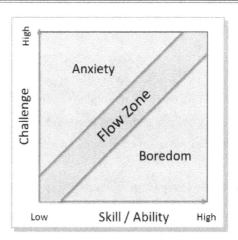

Psychologically, it has been proven time and again that most humans experience the *state of flow* while playing games. A game designer always dreams of creating a game that fully exploits this flow phenomenon. The perfect setting for a flow is achieved only when the player is performing at their optimal skill level or ability. A game should be designed in such a fashion that the *challenge* matches the player's *ability*.

When the challenge level is too high considering the player's abilities, the player experiences too much anxiety or frustration and shies away. In contrast, when the challenge level is not on par with the player's abilities, the player tends to enter the boredom zone and shows huge signs of disengagement. An ideal game should ensure that the challenge matches the player's current ability for the player to enter into the flow zone and gradually groom them over time to gain mastery with practice. The player starts with a small challenge but eventually confronts huge challenges with an inherent desire to upgrade their abilities and become the master.

An employer can exploit game design principles in order to create that flow zone in the workplace and groom their employees to achieve high skill levels and attain highest efficiency levels. With well-defined goals and active feedback loops, an employee can enter into the flow zone whenever they are challenged with an opportunity that matches their inherent potential.

Enterprises have started leveraging this powerful concept of gamification in engaging their workforce, paving the way to a new buzzword called *enterprise gamification*. This refers to deploying gamification within an enterprise to engage and align with the workforce better. The employees are empowered to explore personal strengths, enhance competencies, establish social connections, and attain a sense of accomplishment. The employer, in turn, benefits from the improved productivity, improved service to the customer, and better employee retention. The employer is able to accomplish the desired outcome, keeping the employee engaged to a higher degree.

Approaches to gamification can be broadly bucketed in two major categories:

➤ Process-centric gamification
➤ User-centric gamification

Process-centric gamification

An organization can take up processes within an enterprise and induce game mechanics, dynamics, and aesthetics into the process to make it more efficient and engaging for the users.

Case study – 1

Microsoft used gamification on top of its bug testing engine to encourage non-QA staff to perform bug testing. The company used gamification for language translations in software localization efforts to publicize top contributors.

The impact has been stellar, with 4,500 participants reviewing 500,000 dialog boxes addressing 170 bugs. Particularly, Microsoft Japan took just a single day to weed out all localization errors.

Case study – 2

Cognizant launched an internal platform called OneCognizant (1C) that facilitates business process orchestration through an internal app store with game mechanics and dynamics intertwined to engage its employees.

The impact has been overwhelming, with 10 million user hits, 100,000 likes, and 300 plus apps in the app store, enabling 102 business processes and five engagement channels contributing to a modest increase in employee satisfaction score with three key business processes doubling in user compliance.

User-centric gamification

An organization can launch a gamified initiative to engage and influence the user primarily with the objective of rendering the user more effective and efficient. Typically, this comprises of improving employee wellness and individual productivity.

Case study – 1

NextJump, an offers and rewards company in New York, built its own internal health application that split the company into five teams and rewarded the winning teams for regularly exercising by depositing cash in each team member's health savings account.

The impact has been that 70 – 75% of NextJump's employees work out regularly. This saves the company millions of dollars in work attendance and insurance costs, and makes the workplace healthier and happier.

Case study – 2

Keeping in view the resistance to change and to emphasize the importance of change in management, an initiative called *tiny changes* was floated in my organization. Employees can tweet about a tiny change that they have incorporated in their workplace or personal lives. Every week, a winner would be picked by the CIO.

The employees adopted this initiative big time and started incorporating slight changes in their routine that increased their wellness and created a congenial work environment. Sharing the tiny changes with the community encouraged others to adopt these changes. A few tiny changes incorporated by the associates that went viral are as follows:

> *I started using the staircase instead of the elevator and feel more brisk and refreshed.*

> *I walk over to the desk of my teammates and help them troubleshoot. I derive more satisfaction.*

> *I have started to volunteer for the CSR program and tutor underprivileged children over the weekends.*

Enterprise gamification can benefit organizations in many ways, a significant few being:

> ➤ Improve employee engagement

> ➤ Increase employee productivity

> ➤ Effective problem solving

> ➤ Improve quality of service

> ➤ Drive innovation

> ➤ Enhance synergy and collaboration

> ➤ Increase speed to market

> ➤ Better employee retention

Gamification catalyst for employee engagement

Many times, an employee fails to enter into the flow zone because they don't identify with the goals, so they think, *What is in it for me?* Game mechanics can help bridge that gap in demonstrating that value in an engaging manner.

A well-designed gamification system that lets employees enter into a flow zone by deploying a combination of these mechanics can achieve higher levels of employee engagement.

Game mechanics at enterprises

The following are a few game mechanics and illustrations of scenarios within an enterprise where they may apply:

Game Mechanic	Description	Scenario
Achievements	A virtual or physical indication of having accomplished something.	An employee is rewarded as "Best performer of the month." (can be virtual rewards)
Appointments	A predetermined time or place a user must log in or participate in the game for positive effect.	An employee is expected to complete a knowledge quest on Know your organizational assets or Know your customer, after coming on board.
Behavioral momentum	Tendency of players to keep doing what they have been doing.	An employee continues to play a skill game and gains learning credits even after exceeding the stipulated credits for the annual period.

Game Mechanic	Description	Scenario
Blissful productivity	The feeling of being happy by playing a game and working hard, rather than being idle or relaxed.	An employee volunteers to perform a challenging task and aspires to accomplish the goals with utmost commitment.
Bonuses	Reward after completing a series of challenges or core functions.	An employee is rewarded with performance incentives or spot awards for their delivery excellence.
Cascading information theory	Release information in minimum possible snippets to gain the appropriate level of understanding at each point during a game narrative.	An employee who is an entry level trainee is required to complete the basic level of technology training and gains a beginner badge and is gradually encouraged to learn the advanced curriculum as subsequent levels to gain mastery.
Combos	Reward skills after completing a combination of actions.	An employee is required to complete x hours of attending training sessions and y hours of handling training sessions and complete a certification in order to gain learning credits for the period under consideration.
Community Collaboration	Entire community is rallied to work together in solving a riddle, problem or challenge.	An employee is required to drive their team to win the Best Product Idea award where they work collaboratively with marketing executives and functional and technical analysts.
Countdown	Players are only given a certain amount of time to do something.	An employee is given compensatory leave for a day that needs to be availed within the next 2 weeks.
Discovery	Surprise the players by letting them discover or explore something.	An employee submits an innovative idea and receives an invite for Lunch with the leadership team.

Game Mechanic	Description	Scenario
Epic Meaning	Players will be highly motivated if they believe they are working to achieve something great, something awe-inspiring, something bigger than themselves.	An employee is given the opportunity to lead a huge product venture that could transform the fortunes of the company as part of their diversification roadmap.
Free Lunch	Players feel they are getting something for free due to someone else's hard work.	An employee at junior level has joined a team that wins the Project of the year award, so they feel lucky and blessed to be part of the team and want to contribute more.
Infinite Gameplay	Game that does not have an explicit end as it constantly refreshes the content or the player works towards a static or positive state.	An employee who has completed longer years of service continues to invest their best as they feel part of a continuous learning journey.
Levels	Players are rewarded an increasing value for cumulating points and they have a feeling of moving up the ladder.	An employee is elevated to appropriate roles with clear career growth options in alignment with their competency levels.
Loss Aversion	Influencing player behavior not by reward, but by instituting punishment.	An employee is clearly shown the consequences of violating the code of ethics.
Lottery	Winner is determined solely by chance to create a high level of anticipation.	An employee participates in a referral program where there is a sweepstake to double the referral bonus.
Ownership	Players can create, customize, and control their own characters, items, goods, or other things that strengthens loyalty.	An employee is empowered to manage a small venture within their group, unleashing their creativity.
Points	Numerical value given for any single action or combination of actions.	An employee is rewarded points for maximum contribution in Ask the expert forums in the period under consideration.
Progression	Success is granularly displayed and measured through the process of completing itemized tasks.	An employee is shown their continuous progression in achieving the goals set for the current year in the performance review system.

Game Mechanic	Description	Scenario
Quests	The journey of obstacles a player must overcome.	An employee is thrown the challenge of completing a series of certifications to gain the SME status.
Reward Schedules	The timeframe and delivery mechanisms through which rewards (points, prizes, level ups) are delivered.	An employee is clearly shown the reward guidelines and delivery mechanisms in order to push themselves to compete with their peers and excel.
Status	Rank or level of a player.	An employee is elevated to a higher rank if they perform at a higher level.
Urgent Optimism	Indicates extreme self-motivation with a desire to act immediately to tackle an obstacle combined with the belief that we have a reasonable hope of success.	An employee is highly motivated to tackle a challenging situation in a customer project and upholds their organizational brand and their own repute.
Virality	A game element that requires multiple people to play or that can be played better with multiple people.	An employee launches and popularizes a crowdsourcing initiative and gathers tons of ideas from the rest of the team to deliver continuous process improvements.

Gamification and Gen Y

Earlier in the chapter, we referred to certain changing expectations from the Gen Y/millennials at the workplace. You can observe some interesting correlations of these attributes to playing games, which are as follows:

> **Defy hierarchy**: While playing a game, every player is treated equally. A player is usually appreciated based on the merit of the play they exhibit on the day or moment of play, rather than making it based on past glory or positions.

  A gamified initiative in a workplace can effortlessly create a culture where employees are treated alike and their ideas are welcomed and implemented purely based on merit.

> **Collaborative culture**: Games promote a sense of collaboration between the participant players, more so evident in sports when played as team games comprising of players from diverse cultures representing different regions or countries. They provide avenues for the players to mingle and compete in high spirits. They enable people to understand each other's skills better, socialize, and achieve a common goal.

At the workplace, people representing diverse cultures and backgrounds get together to accomplish common goals within an enterprise. A gamified initiative would help to bring the teams together and for the employees to understand about each other's skills and perform well as a team to achieve a common objective.

➤ **Empowerment and trust**: One of the important qualities that intrinsically motivates a player while playing a game is the autonomy that he/she enjoys in making creative moves based on his/her own instincts and abilities. The player is given the liberty to experiment, take risks, face failures, make adjustments, get better and better with more practice, and finally get to winning ways as he/she gains mastery. When players are entrusted with certain roles, they excel and bring the best out of themselves.

At the workplace, when employees are empowered and entrusted to deliver, they are extremely motivated and engaged in owning up to the tasks. A gamified initiative can provide that exhilarated feeling of creative accomplishment. One example would be to decentralize innovation and generate quality ideas from creative employees across the organization through the deployment of game mechanics.

➤ **Instant feedback**: The most engaging aspect of the game lies in receiving instant feedback. The player can infer the consequences of every move made that lets him/her strategize further moves. Irrespective of the outcomes, the player feels a sense of achievement, especially when they boast of their progress and achievements in the peer network and receive acknowledgement from their close circles.

Any gamified initiative incorporates the feedback element as its core where the progress can be published to the community transparently and recognition can be bestowed on a timely basis.

➤ **Flexible environment**: Games are designed to operate in a flexible and fun environment where the players experience a sense of unforced immersion and relaxation.

A gamified initiative can effectively induce certain elements of flexibility and fun in performing tasks that are otherwise stressful, monotonous, and mundane in nature.

➤ **Sense of purpose**: All games demonstrate a sense of purpose for the players who participate in the game. The purpose could be to attain individual glory, bring honors to the team they represent, or could be a cause of charity. That purpose would drive the players to perform at their peaks.

An employee demonstrates their highest levels of engagement when he/she understands and enrolls in a larger cause. A gamified initiative can help employees in discovering that sense of purpose and the impact of their contributions.

Accelerating engagement among employees

Employers within an enterprise can adopt the best practices taking cue from successful initiatives from both non-enterprise and enterprise context. These initiatives demonstrate real value in effectively deploying gamification as a catalyst for engagement.

Driving behavioral changes

By inducing fun, gamification can drive behavioral change towards positive reinforcement.

Case-study

Fun Theory, an initiative by Volkswagen is changing people's behavior for the better. The initiative goes to prove that the best way to drive behavioral change is to let users take part in activities that are fun to undertake with underlying serious benefits. Users are invited to share fun ideas that would drive good behavior and are rewarded.

Speed Camera Lottery, an idea conceived by Kevin Richardson from USA is implemented at Sweden in collaboration with the National Society for Road Safety where the camera at traffic lights snaps the vehicles that pass by along with their speed levels. The law abiders who follow speed limits enter into a lottery and win rewards that are essentially sponsored by the pool of money collected as penalty from those who violate the speed. Average speed in Stockholm trial decreased from 32 to 25 kilometers an hour.

Similarly an idea submitted by Nevena Stojanovic from Serbia called *Play Belt* ensures everyone uses their safety belt in vehicles. Its only when the seat belt is fastened, the in-car entertainment system is switched on, encouraging the kids to follow rules, which they otherwise ignore. This ensures a positive reinforcement to help people adopt safe driving practices that can save lives.

Takeaways for employers

When it comes to code of ethics, security and compliance matters, employees always show a slack attitude in adhering to the protocols. Employers can take a leaf out of this and deploy such fun theory at workplace to drive behavioral changes in employees, especially when it comes to compliance training that has serious implications but often overlooked by the workforce. In fact, in every job that we perform, if we can figure out the element of fun, the tedious aspects of a job can be masked in a game.

Inducing intrinsic motivation

Through interesting game mechanics, gamification kindles intrinsic motivation to perform an activity.

Case-study

Nike, the sports shoe company is a classic example of how intrinsic motivation can be induced into an otherwise tiresome activity like exercising. The company introduced a Nike+ sports kit, where the users attach a sensor in their shoes to track, store and transmit data on their workouts. This includes monitoring activities like duration, speed, distance traveled, calories burned. As the users exercise, they can set personal workout goals in the iPhone app, tune in to favorite music and receive instant feedbacks on their health progress. The data captured is synchronized with the Nike+ server and in turn displayed at the community website. The user can log in to the website to track their workout data, share with friends in the community and enter challenges.

Nike+ has become a unique product category and pushed competition to emulate its success. Nike+'s online community has more than 2 million active members. All members have run 120 million-plus miles, achieved 240,000 daily goals and earned over 220,000 achievements. This in turn increased their membership and helped in boosting company's overall revenue.

Takeaways for employers

In an enterprise, employees are faced with mundane activities that don't inspire them to stay engaged. A typical example could be a clerical job, mobile marketing or customer service job. In such cases, employers can induce game mechanics to intrinsically motivate the employees by providing instant feedback monitoring their key performance indicators, conduct quests and facilitate employee community interactions.

Seeding corporate social responsibility

Gamification aids in promoting awareness and garnering participation towards sustainability programs targeted at social wellness.

Case-study

Ecoinomy, a software solution company has recently partnered with a utility company to encourage their employees to contribute a portion of their monetary savings to community causes chosen by them. Each employee has an online account and submits ideas on eco-saving opportunities and the amount of money and CO_2 emissions saved are tracked.

Over 25 percent of the staff joined with the pilot scheme and the project, helped save the utility £41,000 in costs and 66 tons of CO_2. An annualized estimate of the savings for each employee active in the scheme came to £350, which translates to a potential £7 million in savings if every employee took up the challenge in the future. £8,000 was donated to local causes and nearly 5,000 actions undertaken.

Takeaways for employers

Gamification and sustainability are becoming synonymous these days and corporate houses are employing the tactic to engage their employee community to contribute towards causes of social good including philanthropy and green revolution. Nearly 70 percent of the employees in any organization, identify with causes of social good, and employers should look to gamify **CSR (Corporate Social Responsibility)** and sustainability programs as this creates a sense of belongingness towards their organization.

Better synergy and collaboration

Gamification drives community collaboration to seek and share knowledge.

Case-study

Enterprise software giant **SAP's Community Network (SCN)**, is one of the early pioneers that adopted gamification to enable its developers, customers, and partners to collaborate within respective communities and share knowledge.

With over 200,000 contributors overall, there are about 1,170 discussions per day with 17,000 likes, 7,000 comments, and 6,000 ratings per day on average. Particularly after upgrading the gamification features last year, content creation, comments, and feedback is reported to be up by 113%, community feedback by 250%, and points up by 147% with over 50% month-over-month increase of badges.

Takeaways for employers

Many organizations have started to build a community of practitioners within an enterprise, where peers can network with each other to share knowledge and ask for expert help in the community forums. In order to gain better adoption of such initiatives and to strengthen them, gamification can help a long way in developing better synergy, as is evident in the case of SCN.

Summary

In this chapter, our intention was to understand about the changing expectations of the new age workforce that when not catered to, leads to employee disengagement. Having analyzed the root causes, we learnt about driving employee engagement the SMART way. Further, we illustrated that gamification can act as a catalyst to attain and sustain the highest degree of engagement levels.

In the next chapter, we will learn how to apply gamification within the organizational business processes to increase employee engagement.

>2

Gamification in Action

Having understood from the previous chapter that gamification can act as a catalyst to accelerate engagement, let's explore the business processes where gamification can be put into action within an enterprise.

In this chapter, we will cover:

> The business processes where gamification can be put into action

> How to apply gamification in a variety of business processes

> The other areas of applicability within an enterprise

Gamification and organizational management

There is a continuum of management levels within an organization that can be broadly classified as strategic, tactical, and operational management. Gamification has to be approached more from a strategic viewpoint and interleaved into the business processes so that it functions as an effective catalyst at the tactical and operational levels.

A typical enterprise comprises of business units that may include:

> Sales and Marketing
> Human Resources
> Finance
> Administration
> Research and Development (R&D)
> Training
> Contact Center
> Information Technology

Each of the business units has well-defined business processes listing the series of tasks and activities performed to produce a specific outcome.

Gamification can be put into action in each of these business units and used to address a few of the following scenarios:

> A new process replaces a traditional process, and there is a challenge faced with change management, or in gathering initial momentum, or adoption from the stakeholders

> A retrospective of the business process outcomes shows it has failed to deliver the desired results due to lack of customers, employees, or partner engagement

> A retrospective of certain activities within a business process shows it is mundane or cumbersome in nature and fails to engage the users

Apart from the individual business units, gamification plays a vital role in enhancing the synergy between the varied units and the organization as a whole.

Gamification and enterprise business processes

Gamification can be put into action in a wide variety of areas within an enterprise, including key business processes and other miscellaneous areas.

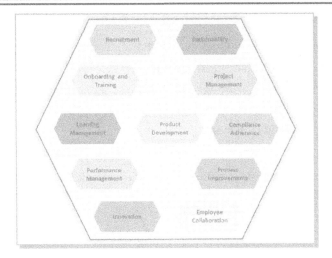

Before deploying gamification as a strategy within an enterprise, let's explore its applicability in some of the key business processes within business units.

Business unit – Sales and Marketing
Business process – Managing salesforce performance
Context

A sales manager is faced with a daunting task to manage and motivate his salesforce. The objectives set by forecasting the annual sales target for the regions under his territory sets the ball rolling for his team. Once the targets are determined, the sales manager has the onus to periodically monitor the performance of his team, provide constant feedback, and take corrective courses of action in the case of aberrations. Every sales team might have a unique demand, and the manager is required to understand their expectations and coach them. The right talent mix has to be aligned to successfully execute the go-to-market strategy. Training and equipping the team with the right tools and technologies helps in creating customer-centric sales pitches and achieving better conversion rates. There is a lot of recordkeeping that needs to be maintained by the salesforce in order to sense those leading indicators that deserve immediate attention. Promoting adherence to processes and adoption of best practices amongst their salesforce is a key challenge faced by sales managers.

Gamification in action

Unlike other areas of business, performance incentives are prevalent in the sales world, and it is difficult for many to appreciate the value that gamification can bring to the table in order to motivate the salesforce.

Typically, a salesforce can be engaged in a SMART way:

> Satisfying them with good performance incentives

> Motivating them with contests and quests

> Advancements in skill through sponsorship of professional training and certifications

> Recognizing them with bonus incentives

> Trusting them to deliver by empowering them

A few of these are executed as individual action items by sales managers already. In order to keep a watch on the overall targets to be accomplished, a holistic view is essential to carefully observe and analyze their behavior and streamline the metrics to track their performance accordingly.

A gamified system helps the sales department to convert a system of transactions to a system of engagement, and can help the sales manager in the following aspects:

> Set clear objectives and targets to track at an individual and team level

> Break the high level tasks into granular activities and track and incentivize at the activity level

> Monitor the key performance indicators or overall metrics and identify and report on the leading indicators that drive the behavior towards good or bad performance

> Seamlessly tie incentives to status tracking to keep the data relevant and up to date

> Gauge progress and provide real-time feedback

> Coach the team with core and soft skills in the form of practical workshops and boot camps

> Organize time-bound and educative contests and quests

> Drive adoption to existing and new initiatives, especially those that involve mundane tasks, like tracking leads, or superiorly challenging tasks, like adoption of new technology and gadgets

> Encourage collaboration with the community to share knowledge and seek expert help, especially when the teams are geographically dispersed

> Facilitate peer and customer feedback in addition to the formal feedback logged by supervisors

Rather than just looking at the sales volume or conversion ratio annually, the sales manager can assess the performance of a sales agent effectively if the progress is tracked by drilling down the high level tasks into a series of granular activities.

A story

Let's assume Mike manages a sales team and they have a gamified system that has **Points, Badges and Leaderboard (PBL)** *in place and also provides a mechanism for the customer to provide feedback ratings:*

Activities	Points	Progress	Prerequisite for awarding points
Cold call	0	10%	
Generate a lead	5	20%	Enter prospect information in CRM system
Illustrate product	25	40%	Update status in CRM system
Close the deal	50	100%	Update status in CRM system

With such tracking in place, sales executive Ryan is encouraged to win points, and also the progress indicator aids him to perform a reality check if he can meet the sales volume targets:

Prospect 1	20%				
Prospect 2	40%				
Prospect 3	100%				
Prospect 4	100%				

Ryan observes his leaderboard and is happy that he is a top performer and stays on course to meet the sales targets:

Probability of meeting sales target	90%
Leaderboard ranking	2
1 more lead will help win	Kudos badge
20 more points will help climb to rank	1

Cyril, another sales executive, is worried about his progress. The system alerts Mike, the sales manager, of Cyril's performance. Mike notices a pattern that Cyril is unable to progress beyond product illustrations to close out a deal. The system performs data analytics and notices a trend that the customers have rated Cyril low on the communication front and augments the notification with this report. This input helps Mike in providing focused coaching to Cyril. Subsequently, this aids in boosting Cyril's skill levels and morale and he can assess his progress in the form of real-time feedback.

Prospect 1	10%				
Prospect 2	20%				
Prospect 3	40%				
Prospect 4	10%				
Prospect 5	20%				

Probability of meeting sales target	30%
Leaderboard ranking	54
Recommended training programs	Communication
10 more points will help climb to rank	53

Inference

This is a basic illustration of how a system of engagement can induce behavioral changes that encourage the users to capture data by tying a tracking mechanism to PBL. Beyond PBL, the system displays a progress indicator to stay focused on accomplishing targets, suggest recommendations for improvement, and notify the appropriate stakeholders supplying valuable insights to necessitate a corrective course of action.

Benefits

> Improve lead generation

> Better conversion ratio

> Shorter sales cycle

> High customer satisfaction

> Enhance skills and achieve mastery

> Better performance tracking

> Better collaboration and synergy

> Increased adoption to existing and new initiatives

Business unit – Human Resources

Business process – Recruitment

Context

A traditional recruitment process confronts a lot of challenges. The decision whether to go in for a full-time employee or to outsource services deserves a special think-tank. The expenses involved in the recruitment processes are huge. This includes the traditional advertising costs, additional costs expended towards conducting occasional job fairs, hiring panels, travel costs for the panels, administrative costs, and so on. The process of shortlisting the right candidates from the varied profile formats is cumbersome. Most CVs in Word document templates submitted by the candidates contain generic statements rather than clarifying specific experience. Since this process becomes inefficient, a lot of time is being wasted in interviewing unqualified candidates. Hiring the right panelists on the day of the interview becomes a challenge considering the availability and nature of skills. Employer brand also matters when it comes to attracting the right talent mix from reputed institutions.

Gamification in action

Gamification can play a pivotal role in hiring the right talent mix as part of the recruitment process. By enrolling the employees to act as advocates, the right talent can be crowdsourced in a timely fashion:

> **Gamify the talent hunt process**: Enterprises have already started gamifying the cumbersome process of recruitment. Marriott International Inc. developed a theme-based online game for players to get a simulated experience of a hotel kitchen manager's work experience. Those who are interested in pursuing a career in hospitality exhibit interest in playing their game on Facebook and the company woos them with interesting career offers.

> **Identify the right talent**: An IT company that looks to recruit geeks can float an online contest for Millennials and toppers can be offered a job. Instead of going through a cumbersome process of scrutinizing profiles with mismatching details, this gives the employer the opportunity to evaluate the right competencies first-hand. These types of contests witness huge crowd participation because of the social reach, and claiming top honors provides the candidates a sense of pride amidst their peer community. Furthermore, they can also pocket a handsome job offer. This would also prove as a branding vehicle for the recruiter, and more importantly save huge cost. Google, Facebook, and IBM deploy such online programming contests to attract and identify the right talent. The same strategy can be used within an enterprise to rotate employees for assignments that better match their skills in order to improve retention.

> **Crowdsource talent**: Instead of recruiting a full-time employee for an assignment, enterprises can look to crowdsource talent from the community external and internal to the organization. Threadless, a Chicago-based t-shirt company, crowdsource t-shirt designs through weekly contests. Customers vote on the designs and winning designs are manufactured every week. This saves huge infrastructure and administrative costs involved in traditional recruitment.

Employees aspire to do certain activities out of interest. At times, these employees could be on the bench awaiting new assignments or more bandwidth. The motivation levels of employees might dip during idle time. They can be allowed to post information on their skills, interests, and availability in the community. The short-term job assignments that typically involve an effort of a week or two can be posted as well in the community by the respective business units and the employees who are interested can volunteer to choose and complete tasks of their interest and win incentives. Publishing a note of appreciation in the community or awarding badges would help engage them.

> ➤ **Benefit through referrals**: Social recruiting and employee referrals are the easier means to spot the right candidates in a quicker timeframe, saving huge advertising costs. Gamification can certainly help in amplifying the effectiveness of a referral program. The common reason for disengagement is because of the lack of fun and timely feedback in the referral process. Most times, employees are kept in the dark about the status of the process, which alienates them from future participation. Also, employees expect something tangible in return for the timely favor apart from PBL (points, badges, and leaderboard). Depending on the stage in which the application is progressing, the role or compensation of the person hired, the availability of skills in the market (if niche), and the immediate demand considering the criticality of the position, a weightage factor needs to be associated and the incentives have to match the efforts.

> ➤ **Crowdsource shortlisting**: The tedious process of shortlisting the right profiles can be eased through crowdsourcing. A community of volunteering panelists can be facilitated who can contribute to the initial scrutiny of applications. Basic incentives can be rewarded matching the quantity and special recognition can be conferred on those who qualify the right candidates on a consistent basis.

> ➤ **Win the loyalty of evaluation panelists**: In order to garner more participation from evaluation panelists, employers should look at connecting and engaging with them on a continuous basis rather than on demand. The recruiters who make significant contributions can be provided with specialized training, sponsored for travel on the hiring day, given a sponsored membership fee for a professional affiliation matching their skills, and so forth. Their contributions can be tracked and highlighted in the performance appraisal. Personalized invites and recommendations can be rolled out to panelists like informing them of an opportunity to hire in their campus and catch up with their old staff members and friends. Alumni volunteering can be promoted, providing a chance for panelists to visit their campus, offer career guidance to the students, and recruit the promising candidates based on demand. Continuous connections can be established between the candidate and the hirer and make their progress transparent. Special recognition can be bestowed on those who consistently spot the top-notch talent.

Benefits

> ➤ Fulfill the demands quickly
> ➤ Improved quality of hiring
> ➤ Improved engagement of panelists
> ➤ Reduced cost
> ➤ Improved employer brand

Business unit – Administration
Business process – Supervising housekeeping services

Context

Almost all commercial enterprises employ housekeeping services comprising of janitors and cleaners, and supervising their work is a herculean task. Some of the challenges include:

> ➤ Maintaining a high quality of cleaning services on a consistent basis

> ➤ Ensuring that the supplies of right equipment, chemicals, dispensers, and others, are in place

> ➤ Ensuring the supplies don't run out of stock

> ➤ Training the housekeeping staff to handle the equipment and supplies appropriately

> ➤ Training the housekeeping staff on being responsive to customer complaints

> ➤ Guaranteeing the proper schedule of cleaning

> ➤ Confirming recordkeeping and maintenance of a checklist

> ➤ Ensuring immediate notification of hazards and protrusions on the floor area or gateway

> ➤ Schedule periodic inspections to perform quality sanitation checks and do regular follow-ups on the corrective course of action

> ➤ Forecast staffing needs and managing absence of staff during festive seasons

> ➤ Keeping the morale of the staff high considering that their wages are low

> ➤ Maintaining a low staff turnover rate

Gamification in action

It is always assumed that gamification has to be implemented only through a sophisticated PBL system. In my point of view, deploying simple game mechanics in a routine task will do the trick to influence one's behavior towards adopting a best practice. Standing by that belief, gamification can be put into action in improving the morale of housekeeping staff and instilling the culture of adopting safety practices:

> ➤ **Gamify checklist**: Every member of the housekeeping staff is expected to maintain an audit checklist of their routine chores. This can be digitized using a kiosk at floor areas where staff can fill in a checklist with simple key presses and the data can be tracked in the backend system. Once a submission is made, messages or icons with positive connotations symbolizing *Congratulations* or *Thank you* can be popped up for the submissions, which might encourage the staff to do proper recordkeeping. Those who submit the checklist regularly and ensure cleanliness consistently for longer periods can enjoy a bonus incentive like an employer sponsoring their child's education.

➤ **Know your floor performance**: Install a ticker display in the floor area that puts a *Thumbs up* icon for the team that keeps their floor most clean. This can be a resultant of the feedback from supervisors or can be tied to the rating or feedback provided by the customers on the floor. This will encourage the entire team to collaborate towards keeping their floors clean.

➤ **Spot inspections**: Surprise elements like spot inspections can be conducted on the floor and those who maintain cleanliness can be sponsored for lunch with their family or provided with compensatory leave or given the liberty to choose the shift times to work on the subsequent week. Since the timing of inspection is unpredictable, excellence might become a habit rather than an act. Those who emerge as top performers can be asked to play the role of an inspector for a day to inspect their peers' work, which might be perceived as an entitlement or a special privilege. Of course, carefully consider the team dynamics and ensure that it does not lead to conflicts.

➤ **Enter wall of fame**: There could be multiple ways in which the housekeeping staff can enter onto a wall of fame where their act of innovation or excellence or vigilance can be recognized and published to a wider audience in the floor area, maybe publishing their photo on an LCD display board or a wall mount and brag about their achievements. A few activities that can gain entry onto a wall of fame may include:

  ➢ Participate in a photo quest where they can photograph a unique aspect they follow towards cleaning that they think is a best practice that their peers should adopt and submit it in a drop box

  ➢ Notify about the hazards and protrusions that can be encountered in the floor area and thereby help in averting big mishaps

  ➢ Notify about the wrong supply of chemicals or dispensers

  ➢ Implementing an environment friendly or *green* initiative at the workplace

  ➢ Putting in long and committed service

➤ **Gamify training**: Fill a room with nonstandard items and train the housekeeping staff to spot them. This will constitute a fun way of bringing about awareness and the toppers can be entitled with a status like *detectives* or *super heroes*.

➤ **Replace supplies regularly**: An unexpected element can be added at the supply area to pick and replace the supplies on a periodic basis like fresh towels and tissue papers. For instance, someone can win a bonus supply pack like an additional towel or an additional hand wash packet, which can be labeled for their personal use.

Benefits

➤ Improved awareness
➤ Encourage better tracking
➤ Encourage safe practices
➤ Improved staff morale
➤ Reduced staff turnover

Business unit – Research and Development
Business process – Managing product development

Context

Quirky, an invention company headquartered in New York, brings innovative products to the marketplace by letting their design staff collaborate with an online community. They initially crowdsource ideas from the online community, solicit votes on the submitted ideas, conduct weekly debates and rate the best ideas, and even approach the community to influence the design of the product right from choosing the design to solving implementation challenges. It is a compelling success story that harnesses the power of gamification to drive innovation. This has a key takeaway for large enterprises looking to exploit the collective intelligence of their employee community and engage them to contribute to new product development.

Gamification in action

A business enterprise can deploy gamification in the product development life cycle right from design, discovering solutions to problems, testing, and even to test the waters with user feedback by letting their R&D team collaborate with the rest of the enterprise community:

> ➤ **Inviting ideas**: The best ideas may not necessarily originate from within the corridors of R&D labs, but can spark from any minds within an enterprise. A system that encourages employees to submit innovative ideas should be in place. Such a system can benefit the employer to leverage the wisdom of the crowd, and empower their employees to think far beyond their chores and solve seemingly impossible problems. The employers can recognize the employees for their contributions, thereby engaging them better by enrolling them into the company's overall vision. Those who contribute the best ideas can be credited as *innovators*.

> ➤ **Building on original ideas**: The entire community is invited to expand on the original ideas and thereby more ideas can multiply from those ideas. All of them who participate towards shaping a basic idea to one of the most powerful innovations can be credited as *innovation partners*.

> ➤ **Convert feedback to ideas**: Sales and marketing executives who invariably stay close to customers gather a lot of useful feedback, and in a traditional arrangement, these ideas might die down before reaching the corridors of R&D teams who work on product development and enhancements. A system that encourages collaboration between the point of sales and product development teams would let the R&D team consume the feedback in the right spirit and incorporate valid suggestions into the product. Since critical feedback is taken with a pinch of salt, gamification can be deployed to pick the brains of sales executives by asking them to participate in ideation campaigns. In such campaigns, the sales executives can mask the user feedback (problems) in the form of an idea (potential solution or opportunity). This way, the sales team would feel more involved in the product development and the R&D team might show more interest in trying out the potential solutions.

> ➤ **Rating best ideas**: A game-like experience is delivered when the community is allowed to rate or vote on the best ideas. The idea is rated based on the feasibility, uniqueness, and business value it delivers to end users, and contributors can be credited as *influencers*.

> ➤ **Solving complex problems**: Foldit, a crowdsourcing game developed by the University of Washington, is a classic example as to how strangers from different sections of the society can come together to solve a complex problem. 46,000 minds came together to solve the secret of a key protein in ten days that eluded the scientists for 15 years.

> R&D teams can always seek out help from the employee community, which could be spread globally across the enterprise, to solve complex problems. Leveraging the community within the enterprise has added advantages in safeguarding the intellectual property within the organization in the case of breakthrough innovations, which might provide the much needed edge over the competition.

> ➤ **Testing**: Testing a product prior to launch and uncovering bugs could be a huge challenge for the R&D teams given the lesser number of people and time they can invest to simulate the infinite possibilities. By enrolling a community and recognizing them for their efforts, testing can be outsourced effectively and the quality of the end product can be significantly improved.

> ➤ **User Feedback**: Before the product is rolled out to the market, there is a huge advantage in testing the waters within the enterprise by inviting a group of employees to enact the role of end users and solicit candid feedback. The feedback can range from commenting on the design aspects to the cosmetic aspects. R&D teams can prioritize the feedback and act upon those that deliver more value. In fact, they can identify the top features that are liked by the community and gear towards initial launch perfecting those features.

Make a note

Caveat: While building a community within an enterprise is commonly prevalent, bringing the employees on board and sustaining their contributions is highly critical to ensure success. Getting the employees to visit the community site and become an active contributor instead of a passive observer is the key challenge faced by organizations. A well-designed gamification system can deliver the goods in driving adoption.

Benefits

> ➤ Increase in speed to market
> ➤ Reduced cost by crowdsourcing
> ➤ Improved collaboration
> ➤ Drive innovation
> ➤ Improved quality of testing
> ➤ Accelerated feedback loops
> ➤ Increased employee loyalty

➤ Solve complex problems

➤ Drive adoption

Business unit – Training
Business process – Imparting continuous learning

Context

When it comes to imparting continuous learning, most organizations rely on classroom sessions or e-learning curriculum either delivered as online verbose courses or serious games where the training is provided through an actual game. Typically, a simulation game is launched to impart training on business processes where the trainees are expected to observe, analyze, and act when challenged with varied scenarios. One such example is PlantVille launched by Siemens, where a plant manager playing the game can get familiarized with the manufacturing process and learn to make key decisions on a variety of issues ranging from energy efficiency to investments in new technology.

That brings our attention to The Khan Academy, a non-profit educational website that has implemented gamification at its best. By organizing the subjects as a constellation map and the lessons branching out from the tree, learning is simplified as a progressive, fun exercise. For instance, learning math becomes a series of logical steps within a network, gradually transitioning from addition to calculus and progressively building knowledge and gradually attaining mastery. Challenges are thrown open and problem solving is approached in the most engaging manner, carefully structured and paced to sustain interest on a continuous basis. Most importantly, the progress is remembered and converted to energy points, and achievements are quantified as meteorite badges worth a pile of accumulated points. This and a series of similar initiatives of gamification have key takeaways for employers to drive continuous learning within the workplace.

Gamification in action

Learning as a pursuit has so many similarities to that of a game. Learning should have the following elements that are equally applicable to games:

➤ Specific goals to accomplish

➤ A game plan to execute

➤ A progressive journey to attain mastery by moving up varied levels

➤ Drive to participate out of voluntary interest

➤ Induce fun

Let's see how a gamified learning system would encourage the associates to set and accomplish continuous learning objectives.

> ➤ **Learning goals**: In the proposed system, specific learning goals are to be set on a periodic basis based on the roles undertaken by the employees and tracked to closure. Instead of rewarding the credits only during closure, the individual activities and intermediate milestones can be identified and appreciated. For instance, identifying the submission of goals on time under varied categories, setting SMART goals, and setting stretch goals are certain activities that can be encouraged through special acknowledgement.

> ➤ **Learning plan**: Creating the learning plan for an employee can be gamified as follows:
>
>> ➤ Recommend a custom learning plan (avoiding too many data entries or navigation paths)
>>
>> ➤ Suggest courses tailored to role and career aspirations
>>
>> ➤ Suggest courses based on peer profiling
>>
>> ➤ Publish feedback or testimony on courses attended and benefits reaped by peers
>>
>> ➤ Complete the plan on time and win credits
>>
>> ➤ Progress indicator charts
>>
>> ➤ Analyze overall progress with respect to completion of learning plan
>>
>> ➤ Compare progress against accomplishing intermediate learning goals
>>
>> ➤ Compare progress against team members

> ➤ **Learning credits**: PMP, a credential from Project Management Institute, has a prerequisite to complete X number of **Professional Development Units** (PDU), typically proportional to the number of hours spent on acquiring the project management body of knowledge. The credential is valid only for the initial Y years, after which it has to be renewed with evidence of continuous learning of completing X number of PDUs in every Y years to follow.

Taking cue from this, setting an annual target of learning credits encourages the employees to pursue learning on a consistent basis while completing their learning plan. Whenever a new course is released, the corresponding learning credits can be displayed and bonus credits can be rewarded for going above and beyond the stipulated credits required to complete the learning plan.

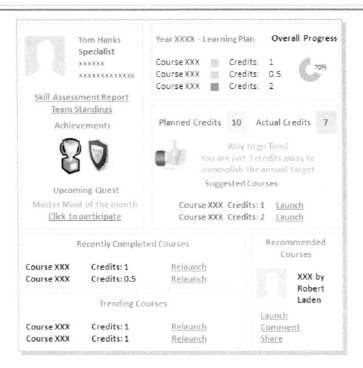

➤ **Learning quests**: Learning quests can be launched to test the skill levels and application of knowledge gained by the employees to accredit their knowledge and elevate them to next levels. The quest can be conducted in the form of a serious game where certain scenarios can be simulated by the employees to test their application knowledge quotient.

➤ **Leveling up**: Career progression and skill upgrades go hand in hand. With every role we undertake, we are expected to demonstrate certain competencies and skills to move up to the next level. Accomplishing the learning goals becomes a key ingredient in preparing us for the new roles. Staying abreast with the latest advancements is equally important to gain a competitive advantage both from an individual and organization standpoint. One way in which continuous learning behavior can be gamified is to level up the employees based on skill upgrades. The trend reports will clearly show the individual's progress over time:

Level	Activities to complete	Status
Level 1	Complete Course 1 (Fundamentals)	Beginner
	Complete Quest 1	
Level 2	Complete Course 1 (Advanced)	Practitioner
	Complete any course from Category 1	
	Complete Quest 2	
	Complete Certification 1	
Level 3	...	Specialist
Level 4	...	Expert

> ➤ When the opportunities are aligned based on status, employees will be more engaged. For instance, *In lieu of this opportunity, we are looking at deploying a Specialist* might encourage the employees to equip adequate skill levels in order to become a Specialist and grab the opportunity.

> ➤ **Endorse skills**: LinkedIn is a classic example to emulate within an organization to establish connections with peers, know about their skill profiles, and endorse skills of peers.

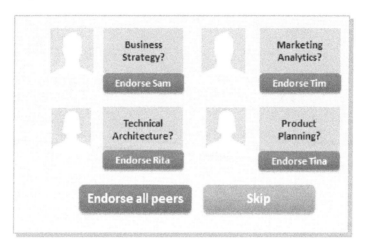

This will indirectly influence the employees to catch up with their peers in terms of upgrading their skills. This information can in turn be used to identify experts in the network and seek guidance or assistance.

> ➤ **Built-in analytics**: The biggest advantage of a gamification system would be the built-in analytics to carry out behavioral analysis on employees, their attitude towards skill upgrades, identify the challenges perceived, and ascertain the skill gaps. It can be leveraged to continuously evolve the system to tailor the process based on those patterns that push the employees to upgrade their skills constantly by personalizing the course recommendations and putting other measures in place based on the insights garnered through analytics.

Benefits

- ➤ Improved productivity
- ➤ Improved quality of service
- ➤ Gain competitive edge
- ➤ Increased employee loyalty

Business unit – Contact Center

Business process – Managing agent performance

Context

If you had to rate tough working conditions associated with a job, contact center/call center operations would figure in the top ten. With rigid work schedules involving weekend and night shifts, frustrated customers voicing non-stop grievances, unrealistic expectations, and targets set by senior management, there is no wonder that these employees get demoralized and disengaged frequently. With the evolution of multiple communication channels, particularly online social networks, expectations from customers with regards to service has rocketed sky-high. Bad customer service experiences can be spread within moments, putting the organization's reputation at stake. The monotonous nature of tasks, poor infrastructure, disintegrated systems with inconsistent reporting, and implementing cost-cutting measures like staff layoffs without proper notice degrades the experience further.

One big challenge faced by the call center management is the huge employee turnover, forcing them to set aside considerably huge budgets in recruiting and training new employees to ensure continuity of service. During the training period, though continuity is manageable, quality of service does take a huge hit. The call center employees represent the face of an organization to the customers during times of need, and it is extremely crucial to get the engagement strategies right. Otherwise, organizations run the risk of losing customers to competition who offer better service.

Gamification in action

There are varied points of disengagement for a call center employee, which include but are not limited to:

- ➤ Assigned a task that is highly boring
- ➤ Assigned a task that is extremely challenging and they do not know where to seek expert help
- ➤ Handling a tough customer who loses their cool and is unwilling to listen
- ➤ Receives only grievance logs as feedback from customers and rarely receives words of appreciation
- ➤ Rarely receives feedback from supervisor on performance

➤ Does not know where they stand with respect to peers or industry benchmarks

➤ Did not receive adequate training to handle the newly launched system

➤ Feel isolated and hardly finds opportunity to collaborate with peers

➤ Lack of tools and resources to perform the tasks productively

➤ Frustrated with inflexible working conditions

The following aspects can be used to address the disengagement factors mentioned previously through the application of gamification. Addressing these factors will in turn help the agent offer better service to customers.

➤ **Learning and Development**: Agent can be provided learning opportunities that include fun elements and provides instant feedback. A few ideas could be as follows:

➢ **Launch quests**: A quest where a virtual customer connects with an agent and he logs his responses. The system analyzes his response and provides a rating on his effectiveness. This will also help to understand the challenges faced by an agent in specific areas and the supervisor can offer tailored coaching.

➢ **Launching new courses**: An agent needs to keep himself updated with the new training modules and by attending and completing these courses on time, they can also win badges.

➢ **Reversal of roles**: An agent can act as a customer and his/her manager can play the role of an agent to let the agent know how it feels with regards to the quality of service offered. The best performing agents can be rewarded. This is a very effective way in which the behavior of an agent can be influenced to empathize more with customers.

➢ **Playback video/audio recordings**: Video should be used as a powerful medium to train agents on handling scenarios. Watching them over and over would give them a sense of confidence in handling tricky callers. *Reversal of role* enactments can be captured as videos and the winner's series can be archived and broadcasted for playback. Similar audio recordings of the best customer interactions (ones recorded with customer consent) can also be effectively used for training purposes, and the best responses can be podcasted in the virtual *wall of fame* series publicizing the names of agents figuring in those conversations.

➤ **Supervisor feedback**: A reporting dashboard with analytics performed on top of the basic KPI and correlating with other behavioral indicators will help the supervisor provide constructive feedback to the agents. For instance, a weekly leaderboard with KPIs tracked can be made transparent to the agent and supervisor. In the case of demonstrated superior performance, the supervisor can attach a template appreciation like *Great work* to the toppers and publicize them to the team. The supervisor can offer his/her coaching help to those whose performance is consistently poor. A dialogue can be triggered in private right from the dashboard establishing an instant connection between both supervisor and the poor performing agent that ensures confidence and support for coaching.

➤ **Customer feedback**: Most times, customers are in an urgency to get their issues solved, and once done, they don't find time to fill-in the two-page survey forms. The system has to gamify means in which customer feedback can be captured in an instant and intuitive manner. A like/dislike button can convey about the overall service and 95 percent of likes would naturally translate to positive experience, motivating the agent to perform better. If only 22 percent of likes is observed, the supervisor can be notified of the trend and face-to-face meetings can be set up to understand the concerns.

➤ **Peer collaboration**: Most agents work in an isolated world, and it is extremely important to enroll them into the team culture and provide them a platform where they can collaborate with other team members. Be it in the physical space or in the virtual platforms, building a community where they can share knowledge, share their good/bad experiences, seek expert/peer help to handle tough situations, watch videos on how to handle different scenarios, and conduct campaigns and polls would motivate the agents to keep themselves engaged and inspired.

➤ **Flexibility perks**: The points accumulated by call center agents for good work on certain stipulated periods can be redeemed through innovative means like picking up a flexibility option. Rather than being merely monetized, such twists keep the employees guessing and push them to participate. This will help them engage in certain activities to earn that flexibility. For instance, an employee delivering superior performance during December can be provided a two day holiday extension during Christmas. Such flexibility perks are head fake strategies to be deployed by the management to sustain continuous engagement by rewarding good work with unanticipated incentives. This will improve the overall performance of the team in anticipation of flexibility perks.

Make a note

Caveat: Gamification works as an engagement strategy if and only if the executive and middle management get the basics right. If the organization fails to improve on basic working conditions, ensure the right infrastructure, the right tools and technologies, the right resources, and the right encouragement and support from the supervisors, any strategy that is deployed to improve engagement also fails to deliver.

The wider adoption of gamification in call centers is testified by the success of exclusive platforms like PlayVox from Arcaris that gamifies the contact center by driving sales and customer service performance. LiveOps, a cloud-based call center platform, is another classic example to testify the power of gamification. By partnering with Bunchball, LiveOps transformed the customer service experience by improving service levels, improving the recruitment of agents, and enhancing overall sales performance.

Benefits

- ➤ Improved productivity
- ➤ Improved service levels
- ➤ Improved employee morale
- ➤ Increased collaboration
- ➤ Better customer satisfaction
- ➤ Reduced staff turnover

Other key areas of applicability

There are many other areas in which gamification can be put into action in the purview of an organization as an effective strategy for engagement. Some of the generic areas include:

- ➤ Employee collaboration
- ➤ Process improvements
- ➤ Compliance adherence
- ➤ Project management
- ➤ Sustainability

Employee collaboration

The employees of an organization are typically widespread across geographies and regions, and having a virtual collaboration platform helps in establishing synergy between the varied teams and individuals. In order to drive the adoption of such platforms, especially in hierarchical organizations where communication usually flows through the hierarchy, introducing game mechanics comes in handy. **Yammer** is a popular collaboration software that helps in sharing ideas or information across teams within the organization and also increases interactions within project teams in order to get work done and arrive at prudent decisions after hearing multiple perspectives.

With Badgeville integration, Yammer enjoys increased adoption as users are equipped with gamification features like gaining virtual rewards, opportunities to socialize their achievements, embracing ideation, and rating tools.

Process improvements

Organizations strive to create a culture of continuous process improvements in order to deliver better value to their customers. Identifying and fixing process gaps, re-engineering legacy processes, automating redundant processes, reusing valuable assets, and sharing best practices are some of the key behaviors promoted in order to increase the process efficiency, thereby driving employee productivity and in turn providing enhanced customer experience. Gamification can produce desirable results in promoting such behavior and provide real-time feedback to all parties involved.

Compliance adherence

Compliance adherence is one area that is often despised or discarded by the employees. Neither do they like to go through the tedious procedure nor do they attach enough importance to the process, but the good news is that gamification can come in handy. Two areas where it commonly applies include compliance training and timesheet submission.

True Office, a startup, offers an interactive gameplay and immersive storyboards that transform mandatory compliance training into a fun, intelligible, and quantifiable experience. This is accomplished by engaging employees to encounter complex, everyday business situations and understand risk-sensitive compliance issues. Building an advanced analytical engine on top of the serious game, they assess the employee's attitude towards compliance and accordingly discern the high risk individuals. By distinguishing the employees who have completed the training from those who haven't or by awarding badges to those who promptly complete compliance training on time and sharing the achievements, the rest of the community can be encouraged to complete the training.

Timesheet submission is also another area where employees are encouraged through gamification to submit timesheets. Some of the strategies include:

➤ Reward badges to individuals and teams

➤ Share achievements with peers

➤ Emphasize the importance through simple quests

➤ Provide real-time feedback on compliance levels and relative standings for both individuals and teams

Slalom Consulting has incorporated this idea in the name *Promptitude*, a user-friendly tool to encourage their employees to complete the time entries by weekends, which tasted success.

Project management

Application of gamification to project management is still in nascent stages. RedCritter Tracker claims that they are one of the one of the first companies to gamify Agile project management, where task execution is rewarded with points, badges, leaderboard, and Twitter-style feeds for projects. This resonates well with the millennial generation who would like to work in a system of engagement where they can establish social connections with the team members and supervisors just as they operate in the social networks to nurture interpersonal relationships. *Propstoyou* is a similar project management tool that relies on motivational theory to maximize team productivity. Like other gamification systems, this has points and badges, but instead of concentrating on a leaderboard with relative ranking, this primarily emphasizes on rewarding an individual's path to mastery and promotes team collaboration through network connections.

Sustainability

Gamification is emerging as a key weapon in sustainability programs, and organizations nudge their employees to adopt sustainable practices in line with their corporate social responsibility agenda. While some of them promote a better lifestyle mainly focused on health and wellness initiatives, some engage in charity while a few others promote environmental awareness. Walmart provides a royalty-free license to organizations interested in adapting **My Sustainability Plan** (**MSP**) for their employees or stakeholders. Here, employees can voluntarily create and track MSP goals and their progress. Two million employees are challenged to commit to a change to make their life, or that of the planet, a little bit better. Such eco-friendly initiatives create a sense of responsibility towards the community and develop a strong bonding towards the organization.

There are a few evidences of people experimenting with gamification in core business processes like master data management, customer relationship management, and business process management. This goes to show that gamification continues to attract attention permeating across the layers of an enterprise.

Summary

In this chapter, we learnt how to put gamification into action within varied business processes and thereby improve employee productivity, reduce employee turnover, improve sales performance, bring about better collaboration, and improve quality of service to customers.

In the next chapter, we will delve deep to understand the steps involved in devising an enterprise gamification strategy.

3
Enterprise Gamification – Strategize

Welcome to the real gameplay. It's time to dig deep and understand the need for an enterprise gamification strategy and the means to put together a strategy.

In this chapter, we will cover:

> - Why is there a need for an enterprise gamification strategy?
> - What are the steps involved in strategizing enterprise gamification?

The need for an enterprise gamification strategy

Humans are often caught up by herd mentality, influenced by their peers to adopt certain behaviors and practices. Businesses are not an exception as they meticulously follow trends adopted by their peers with the concern of being left out. Most enterprises started enrolling themselves into gamification after it figured in Gartner's hype cycle for emerging technologies. After enjoying much hype and attention in 2012, gamification's fortunes were clearly at stake with Gartner predicting that by 2014, 80 percent of gamified applications will fail to meet the business objectives primarily due to poor design. The following are reasons for which it could go wrong:

> ➤ Gamification thought of as an *elixir* to cure all the problems with respect to user engagement

> ➤ Devising disparate strategies to squeeze gamification that seldom align with the overall business objectives

> ➤ A dearth of skilled professionals to design good gamification systems by understanding and applying the gaming principles

> ➤ Implementing gamification as a cosmetic layer on top of the existing systems and processes

> ➤ Failing to understand the behavior and expectations of the target audience

A gamification strategy is a prerequisite in order to avoid the common pitfalls just listed. We already saw in *Chapter 2, Gamification in Action,* that gamification has to be approached more from a strategic viewpoint and interleaved into the business processes so that they function as an effective catalyst at the tactical and operational levels.

Having an effective strategy in place could make all the difference to avoid failure, if not guarantee success. Any organization looking to deploy gamification can approach it with the following four-point agenda:

> ➤ Strategize

> ➤ Design

> ➤ Implement

> ➤ Sustain

The following is a summary of steps covered in each of the phases:

Strategize	Design	Implement	Sustain
■ Defining the business objectives ■ Identifying the target audience ■ Understanding the target audience behavior ■ Validating the business case for gamification	■ Understanding design thinking ■ Researching ■ Ideating ■ Prototyping ■ Testing	■ Selecting the right gamification platform ■ Defining the roadmap for pilot implementation ■ Building the system ■ Measuring and monitoring outcomes ■ Scaling from pilot to full-blown launch	■ Sustaining outcomes ■ Developing adoption strategies ■ Seeding the culture

In this chapter, we will cover the first phase, **Strategize**, followed by the next three in the subsequent chapters.

Defining the business objectives

Before deciding whether gamification should be deployed to amplify the desired outcomes, the maiden step in the Strategize phase is to define the *business objectives* that the enterprise is trying to accomplish.

Defining the high level objectives

To start with, list the high level business objectives as aspirations.

Examples of high level business objectives could include:

1. How can we encourage reuse of assets within the enterprise?
2. How can we increase the quality of service to customers?
3. How can we increase adoption of the new technology initiative recently launched?
4. How can we get people on board sooner in department X?
5. How can we encourage our employees to be compliant?
6. How can we lower the cost of maintenance?
7. How can we ensure the scalability and portability of the computing platform?
8. How can we decrease time-to-market for product rollouts?
9. How can we reduce the infrastructure cost?
10. How can we improve the security interfaces for end user systems?

You can recall from *Chapter 2, Gamification in Action*, that, gamification does have applicability in augmenting the outcomes of a few of the business objectives mentioned earlier (1 – 5), while deploying gamification in a few other scenarios might prove ineffective on the face of it (6 – 10).

Let us take the first high level objective from the list and investigate further as we think gamification can fit the bill.

How might we encourage reuse of assets within the enterprise?

Typically in IT organizations, there are diverse groups that are geographically spread and operate in large team sizes. While a large number of software assets (source code, proposals, project artifacts, and so on) are created by the employees, adoption and reuse of those assets is poor.

The wish list with respect to adoption and reuse of assets is huge:

> ➤ What if I am able to pull out a similar proposal response that addresses the complex business problem I am trying to solve?

> ➤ What if I am able to rapidly set up the customer application with a bootstrap framework?

> ➤ What if I am able to reuse a compliant in-house tool that performs data migration between two data sources within my enterprise?

> ➤ What if I am able to adopt the design and coding standards recommended by my enterprise architecture group?

> ➤ What if I am able to access the research report in the subject area that I am newly exposed to?

> ➤ What if I am able to identify an expert and seek their advice in the subject matter concerned?

Most of this data is not available in the public domain for reuse. It is subject to access control as it constitutes confidential and sensitive information within the boundaries of an enterprise. Typically, employees exhibit slackness in publishing or updating these assets in a common repository so that it is available for reuse by their colleagues. Even when it comes to consumption, the engagement level is poor with respect to adoption of best practices and so employees end up reinventing the wheel.

Reuse of assets can provide lot of benefits that include:

> ➤ Increased productivity

> ➤ Quicker onboarding and training

> ➤ Reduced efforts

> ➤ Huge cost savings

> ➤ Rapid development

- ➤ Enhanced quality (as it's already tested)
- ➤ Enhanced collaboration
- ➤ Expert identification

With so many benefits under the belt, there are no evident motivators to promote reuse. Let's evaluate whether gamification can help.

Framing the SMART goal

Let's convert a high level objective to a **SMART** goal (**Specific**, **Measurable**, **Achievable**, **Realistic** and **Time-bound**).

Specific: *What do you want to achieve?*

Promote reuse of assets.

Measurable: *How much do you want to achieve?*

A 20 percent productivity improvement and onboarding time reduction of 2 days.

Achievable: *How can the goal be achieved?*

By identifying the process gaps and specific motivators.

Realistic: *Is it relevant in the context and realistic to pursue?*

Yes.

Time-bound: *By when it should be achieved?*

Q4 this year.

SMART goal statement: *Goal statement has to be like a command or an instruction. By identifying the process gaps and deploying specific motivators, it promotes the reuse of assets.....of 2 days. By identifying the process gaps and deploying specific motivators, promote the reuse of assets within an enterprise and aim to achieve 20 percent productivity improvements and an onboarding time reduction of 2 days.*

Listing the pain points

Once the SMART goal is framed, list the *pain points* faced in the current business context.

Make a note

You can find the actual meaning of *pain points* at: http://www.waywordradio.org/pain_point/

After analyzing the existing business processes and the enterprise systems, we gather that there could be many pain points acting as a hindrance to achieving the goal. Some of them are listed as follows:

1. Disintegrated platforms
2. Intricate workflow to publish and approve the assets
3. No mechanism to validate the appropriateness of assets
4. Version maintenance challenges
5. Access control and confidentiality concerns
6. Poor user experience
7. Lack of ownership
8. Lack of motivation

Grouping the action items

After listing down the pain points, prepare a list of high level action items required to address the pain points and group them.

There are three key areas in which the business capability of the organization needs to scale up in order to achieve a business goal. They include:

➤ Process

➤ People

➤ Technology

Here we identify the typical areas of improvement and bucket the action items in each of the three facets as follows:

Pain points	Action items		
	Process	**People**	**Technology**
1 – 5	Establish a new process workflow and policy guidelines for reuse	Identify owners and users and orient them on the new process	Launch an integrated platform to publish / consume assets
6 – 8	Establish a process to improve user experience and incentivize reuse.	Engage employees, promote reuse, and drive adoption	Induce gamification elements in the system

We move on to step 2 in the Strategize phase to check whether gamification can potentially help in amplifying the desired outcomes toward accomplishing the business objectives.

Identifying the target audience

Identifying and understanding target audience behavior is one the most critical steps before validating the business case for gamification. Any gamification strategy can succeed only when the business objectives and the user objectives overlap. A user is usually referred to as a **player** in the gaming context. While talking of player types, we are naturally reminded of Richard Bartle and the *Bartle test* that was created by Erwin Andreasen and Brandon Downey, based on a paper written by Bartle.

Perceiving the player types

Bartle's test identifies four types of game players as depicted:

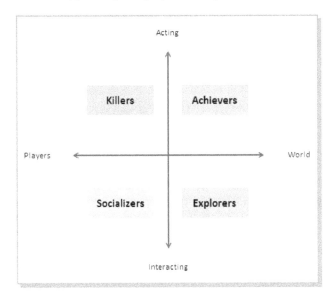

> ➤ **Achievers**: They seek rewards and would be inclined to accumulate points and climb higher levels because of the pride associated with the achievements.

> ➤ **Explorers**: These players are more of the adventurous kind who love to discover things by traversing through uncharted territories or love to uncover something that is hidden.

> ➤ **Socializers**: Socializers derive lot of pleasure through cooperation as they look forward to building interpersonal relationships by interacting with the community.

> ➤ **Killers**: These kinds of players thrive on competition, dominate the show, and derive more pleasure from beating others in the path to victory.

Though each of us might have a mix of all these characteristics in varied degrees and might behave differently in different circumstances, one of the characteristics might slightly dominate the rest.

Classifying employees as players

When it comes to classifying the employees in a workplace who represent the target audience of a gamification system, it won't be as straightforward as Bartle player types. Still, this emphasizes the fact that a good gamification system should be designed keeping the audience personalities and their characteristics in mind. It should have some key attributes embedded within that cater to all types of players, in this case the employees, in order to keep them glued.

Understanding the target audience behavior

The most effective way to drive user engagement is by understanding the behavior of your target audience. There are many ways in which the employees within an organization can be classified in order to decide what could best motivate and engage them. Some of them include:

> Industry type/Profession

> Generation type/Age

> Designations/Roles

> Primary skills and attitude

> Pastime interests

> **Industry type/Profession**: The employees vary by the industry type they represent and the nature of activities that their profession warrants. For instance, an insurance industry is driven by strict norms and regulations that an employee in the insurance industry might be more conservative compared to an employee representing the IT industry. Even within a similar industry, a medical sales representative might come from an informal, flux environment compared to another healthcare professional in a formal environment. It is essential to understand the culture of the employees and weave the gaming elements around that culture even in a non-game context. Otherwise, change management would be extremely tough, forcing the employees to move out of the flow zone either pushing them to anxiety or boredom.

> **Generation type/Age**: In *Chapter 1, Employee Engagement and Gamification*, we already dealt with understanding the employee needs and expectations of varied generations in the workplace. Going by the Bartle's player types, baby boomers in senior executive positions have more shades of *Achievers* who can be motivated by the pride and status. Gen X are more of the middle managers who are *Explorers* and can be engaged if they are provided avenues to explore. Gen Y are more of the *Socializers* who have thrived on the social media culture outside of their professional world and want to replicate a similar culture at the workplace too. They are highly motivated by establishing social connections and like to share their achievements with their peers. All generations might contain very few *Killers*.

➤ **Designations/Roles**: While every organization could have a multitude of designations and roles and it is difficult to spell them out, the roles can be broadly classified into three levels:

> ➢ **Senior leaders**: It might be presumed that the senior level executives within an organization might not need an engagement program compared to junior level staff. On the contrary, the impact of a senior member quitting an organization is quite high and could prove detrimental to the future of an organization. The organizations have to think beyond PBL and concentrate on broader aspects when it concerns the engagement of its senior leaders. The following are some activities to observe:

Engage them with pet projects: Many senior leaders would love to experiment with pet projects at the later stage of their career and any opportunity provided to them to mentor, coach, and guide the employee community would keep them intrinsically motivated.

Nominate for recognition in the industry: The organization should institute appropriate recognition for their senior leaders not just within the organization but also nominate them for recognition in the *global corporate* sector.

Actively participate in gamification initiatives: It is important that the organizations have a buy-in from their senior leaders to actively participate in the gamification initiatives in whatever capacity they can. By participating in an open and collaborative culture, they can in turn engage the employees and build trust factor.

> ➢ **Middle managers/Supervisors**: Middle managers or supervisors tend to be the people who get sandwiched between senior leaders and operatives and can be influenced by the disengagement factors that they discern at both ends. At times, the nature of their work might get mundane, pushing them out of the flow zone to boredom. It is extremely essential to keep this community engaged as they play a key role in maintaining the motivation levels of operatives high. If a supervisor fails to establish basic levels of trust with an employee, any efforts at gamification will almost always fail. As highlighted in the case of senior leaders, middle managers should be provided with specific opportunities to acquire specialization skills, mentor employees, and be nominated for institutional recognition programs.

> ➢ **Operatives**: Most of the employee engagement initiatives including gamification are directly targeted at the ground level employees of the organization as they form the core of the business operations. While the junior level operatives attach higher importance to acquiring skills and monetary perks, the senior level operatives yearn for status and pride. The gamification initiatives need to strike a balance in terms of reward mechanisms while catering to the expectations of the diverse nature of operatives at the varied stages of their career.

> ➤ **Primary skills and attitude**: Each employee possesses primary skills and exhibits a certain attitude at work. Some may be highly analytical but reticent. Some may be moderately skilled but extremely committed. Some may possess the drive to win and flair to lead. Some may be excellent with coordination and communication. By understanding the basic profile of a person, their skills and attitude combined, their behavior can be transformed by nudging them to perform activities aligned with their optimal abilities, ultimately pushing them to the flow zone. A person with good communication would naturally be an active participant in a collaborative environment whereas the person with high analytical thinking might be more engaged to participate in a competitive quest.
>
> Taking cue from online shopping sites, the gamification system if powered by analytics can do this job effectively in providing personalized recommendations. If you have ever done online shopping, you can actually observe that the system remembers what we browsed last and throws up a few recommendations, automatically matching those category of items. For instance, if you are a regular book buyer, it shows up the latest books from your favorite genre. Likewise, a gamification engine can help you interpret the attitude or personality type of the employee and engage them in activities that let them exploit their strengths. On the flip side, any indifference in attitude or aberration from the norm can also be notified by the system, enabling the supervisor or concerned authorities to further analyze the reason behind the deviance.

> ➤ **Pastime interests**: An often ignored but very powerful means to engage employees is to identify their pastime interests and provide them with an opportunity to pursue their interests at work. This is the best form of intrinsic motivation that can be provided to an employee to indirectly enhance their productivity—as a measure in performing their regular jobs efficiently.
>
> Interpreting and comprehensively recording target audience behavior is formally facilitated as part of the research activity in the design exercise that will be discussed in *Chapter 4, Enterprise Gamification – Design*.

A story scenario

I would like to narrate a personal story of engagement at my workplace. Seven years ago, I was introduced to the corporate blogging platform in my organization. It all started as a pastime activity and slowly transformed into a passionate activity that in turn created a sense of belonging toward the organization and its goals.

This blogging platform was launched as part of the Enterprise 2.0 initiative where the employee community was expected to collaborate with each other and share knowledge.

In order to drive adoption, a few engagement strategies were adopted, the significant ones being:

> ➤ The employees were allowed to write posts on any topic of personal interest apart from the significant business posts (within the bounds of decorum of course)

> ➤ Provided x incentives for publishing posts that when accumulated can be redeemed for goods

> ➤ Provided three times the incentives for publishing posts of business significance

> ➤ The senior leadership team including the CXOs were brought to the platform to share key announcements and updates to the employees

> ➤ On a monthly basis, top blog posts from each community were chosen, and the winning posts published to the global audience (influenced by usage statistics and picked by experts)

> ➤ Annual rewards were instituted to honor the top bloggers (voted by the community and experts)

During the initial days, my key drivers of personal motivation (extrinsic and intrinsic) included:

> ➤ The opportunity to be self-expressive

> ➤ To publish posts of personal interest

> ➤ The ability to gain incentives

> ➤ To discover like minds

> ➤ To obtain comments from peers

> ➤ To connect with co-workers who are geographically wide-spread

Over a period of time, I could sense that the motivation transformed to purely intrinsic and finally reached the optimal engagement zone:

> ➤ To follow senior leadership posts

> ➤ To identify with organizational initiatives and goals

> ➤ To contribure towards accomplishing the organizational goals

> ➤ To develop a sense of belonging in the organization

> ➤ To publish considerable posts with business significance apart from personal interests

> ➤ To share knowledge with the community

> ➤ To identify and connect with subject matter experts in respective communities

> ➤ To discover new opportunities

The platform allowed the employees to connect with peers and leaders from different locations, understand broader perspectives, bring forth issues to the concerned department, gain visibility to thought leaders, invite feedback on personal or professional forays, gather support towards sustainability initiatives, and pave the way to infinite other possibilities.

Albeit this initiative was not tagged under gamification, I personally underwent the behavioral transformation of being part of a journey that shifted from extrinsic motivation to intrinsic motivation to driving deeper levels of engagement.

In fact, over a period of time, the platform was owned by the employees themselves where they started gamifying the system to influence and engage their respective communities. A good gamification system should let the employees adopt the system as their own, ensuring deeper levels of engagement, and also keep evolving with time, providing a fresh outlook while sustaining the outcomes the system is devised for.

Validating the business case for gamification

Prior to validating the business case for gamification, let's spend a few moments in understanding the transformation of enterprise systems in recent times and the position of gamification in these systems.

Understanding the system of engagement

Organizations have primarily relied on the system of records or transactional systems modeled on a structured workflow, to deliver the functionality as desired by the user. The user expected the system to deliver an intended functionality by responding within a stipulated timeframe. With the surge of social media, smartphones, big data, and cloud technologies, the system and the data are *loosely structured* and are expected to deliver an experience to the end user, rather than a mere functionality. Users leave their digital footprints in a global network and drive huge chunks of conversations that generate business insights. These insights can be interleaved back to the system dynamically to deliver an experience that excites the user. In a way, the user augments the underlying data and expects the system to understand and fulfill their needs implicitly.

The system of engagement can be envisioned to have the following key characteristics:

> Provide user-centric experience, rather than mere functionality
> Provide dynamic and real-time responses
> Mash structured and unstructured information to garner insights
> Facilitate social connections and sharing
> Offer personalized recommendations and services

Ultimately, the goal of the system of engagement is to engage the end user while being agile and adaptive. It has to effectively answer the question that every user asks: *what is in it for them?*

How can gamification help?

Though it is relatively easy to build and design a system of engagement from the ground-up, the system of records cannot be completely shunned in large enterprises, because the organization has definitive targets to meet while operating in a highly regulated environment comprising well-defined processes, workflows, and policies. The organization needs a facelift where the structured processes lend themselves to integrate with the unstructured conversations generated by the user community and deliver a personalized, connected, engaging experience to the end user. Gamification can be thought of as a stimulant that is injected into the process workflow at strategic places to induce employee engagement rather than being a layer on top. It has to be treated as a *makeover* strategy rather than being *makeup*.

In *Chapter 2, Gamification in Action*, we saw that gamification can be put to action in each of the business units to address a few of the following scenarios:

➤ A new process replaces a traditional process and there is a challenge faced with change management or in gathering initial momentum or adoption from the stakeholders

➤ A retrospective of the business process outcomes show it has failed to deliver the desired results due lack of customer, employee, or partner engagement

➤ A retrospective of certain activities within a business process shows it is mundane or cumbersome in nature and fails to engage the users

Formulating the hypothesis

Continuing the previous example, we feel that gamification could address pain points 6, 7, and 8, to promote reusability. We proceed to formulate the hypothesis as follows: *Deploying gamification will promote asset reuse.*

Gathering the data

An ideal gamification system is one that produces high impact on both business goals as well as user behavior. Gather data within your organization to validate the hypothesis that gamification can prove useful in the context of reuse.

Some of the commonly used group creativity techniques include:

➤ Stakeholder interviews

➤ Brainstorming

➤ Brainwriting

➤ Focus groups

➤ Ideation workshops

Analyzing data

Once the data is gathered, analyze the data to prove or disprove the hypothesis. Any structured analysis techniques can be used based on the current maturity level in your organization and based on the quality of data available to arrive at prudent decisions. Some of the analytical techniques that are useful to validate a business case include:

> ➤ Force field analysis
> ➤ Cost-benefit analysis
> ➤ Impact analysis

We choose **Force field** analysis for our discussion as it is one of the techniques more suited in the context of gamification as it involves change management.

Force field analysis

Force field analysis determines the forces that drive towards a goal indicating positive reinforcement, or move away from the goal indicating hindrance or resistance.

The following are the steps involved:

> ➤ Describe the proposal for change
> ➤ List the forces for change in the left-hand side
> ➤ List the forces against change in the right-hand side
> ➤ Assign scores from 1 – 5 (1 being weak and 5 being strong)
> ➤ Consider the forces: benefits, change management, users, cost, assumptions, dependencies, constraints, risks, and so on

The visual representation guidelines are as follows:

> ➤ Draw a central box indicating the proposal for change
> ➤ Jot down the forces within pointed arrows on both sides.
> ➤ The bigger the influence of the force, the bigger the size (width) of the arrow
> ➤ Assign the score outside the arrow
> ➤ Jot down the total on both sides

The analysis can be repeated over and over until we find means to strengthen the forces for the change or means to weaken the forces against the change and the scores can be adjusted accordingly before arriving at a decision.

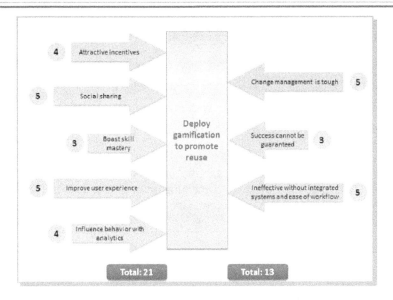

Making the go / no-go decision

Based on the scores computed, we conclude that the forces for the change dominate and gamification fits the bill.

Make a note

Caveats: If we try to squeeze gamification that doesn't have as much impact to business goals, the efforts might fail. Also remember that gamification can solve only specific problems. In the case under discussion:

- If we plan to address pain points 1 – 5 through gamification, the efforts might fail.
- If we fail to address pain points 1 – 5 and address 6 – 8 alone, the efforts might fail.

At the start of the chapter, we observed that most gamification efforts fail and one of the reasons being the mindset that gamification is an elixir to solve all problems.

Let's observe another example. Consider that an organization has a SMART goal statement: *By next quarter, refine the existing process to ensure that the timesheet compliance moves from 65 percent to 90 percent.*

By glancing at the SMART goal, we gather that the organization attempts to increase the timesheet submission compliance levels.

After analyzing the existing business processes and gathering feedback from the employees, the major pain points are listed as follows:

> ➤ Employees are required to log timesheet entries in multiple systems redundantly

> ➤ The enterprise system doesn't scale when concurrent users log in

> ➤ The general response time of the system is very slow

> ➤ The user interface is not intuitive and involves too much navigation

Before proceeding further, we observe that the majority of these bottlenecks pertain to the system performance. In this case, gamification or any alternate technique for that matter will fail to engage the employees if the fundamental issues are not addressed. The organization must fix all the fundamental issues before looking at deploying gamification as a strategy to accelerate engagement levels.

A quick recap

Let's quickly recap all of the steps involved in devising a strategy:

> ➤ Defining business objectives

>> ➢ Defining the high level objective

>> ➢ Framing the SMART goal

>> ➢ Listing down the pain points (halt here if you think there are fundamental flaws to be addressed)

> ➤ Grouping the action items (process, people, and technology, under *Grouping the action items* section, earlier in the chapter) to address pain points

> ➤ Identifying the target audience (employees in this case)

> ➤ Understanding the target audience behavior (particularly with respect to engagement)

> ➤ Validating the business case for gamification

>> ➢ Formulating the hypothesis

>> ➢ Gathering data

>> ➢ Analyzing data

>> ➢ Making the go/no-go decision

The validation checklist

Before proceeding with the design, prepare a checklist and verify that you have the right strategy in place. The following is a sample checklist:

Checklist	Response (Yes/No)
Have you identified the high level business objective?	Yes
Have you decomposed the high level objective to a SMART goal?	Yes
Do you think value provided by gamification aligns with the high level business goal?	Yes
Do you think there are alternate techniques that can influence user behavior and deliver the desired outcome?	No
Have you collected and analyzed enough data to validate the hypothesis?	Yes
Have you identified the target audience?	Yes
Do you have a solid understanding of the behavior of your target audience?	Yes
Are you planning to finalize on the gamification approach and proceed with design after evaluating your target audience?	Yes
Have you identified the Key Performance Indicators to measure performance?	Yes
Do you think gamification can drive those metrics?	Yes

Make a note

Ideally it will help to define each of the KPIs and metrics as part of the validation checklist. Those details are abstracted now. We will be discussing KPIs and metrics in *Chapter 5, Enterprise Gamification – Implementation*.

Summary

In this chapter, we learned how to align gamification with the business objectives. We also learned the importance of identifying and understanding the target audience behavior in order to tailor the system based on their needs and expectations. Overall, we devised a strategy to validate the business case for gamification.

In the next chapter, we will learn how to design a gamification system by applying design thinking approach.

4

Enterprise Gamification – Design

Keeping in mind Gartner's predictions that by 2014, 80 percent of the gamified applications will fail to meet business objectives primarily due to *poor design*, in the previous chapter, we learned about the strategic approach to gamification. We actualized how business objectives must overlap with the user objectives. Let's further explore the kernel of any gamification system, in other words, its design phase.

In this chapter, we will cover:

> - What is design thinking?
> - Why should we apply design thinking to gamification?
> - What are the steps involved in the design thinking process?

Understanding design thinking

While, traditionally, we are used to analytical thinking that involves solving problems for the given context through deductive reasoning, design thinking goes a step beyond this by designing systems intuitively with a human touch. According to Wikipedia's definition

> *As a style of thinking, design thinking is generally considered the ability to combine empathy for the context of a problem, creativity in the generation of insights and solutions, and rationality to analyze and fit solutions to the context.*

Design thinking is a perfect blend of creativity and logic. Again, just like gamification, this is not a newfound concept. Quoting one of the earliest examples, you might be aware that Edison was neither the first nor the only scientist to research on incandescent electric lamps; there were many others. Edison zeroed in on a high resistance system that would require far less electrical power compared to what was commonly used for the arc lamps rendering it suitable for residential use. He discovered the huge market potential of his product by emphasizing how it would serve to lighten up the homes of many in comparison to sticking to conventional notions of commercial use.

Steve Jobs, one of the greatest innovators of all time, had the uncanny ability to design products that are intuitive and end user friendly. The ability of Steve to predict consumer behavior assisted him to script a unique marketing philosophy that put Apple on the map of forward-thinking companies.

Design thinking defines the ideal state and the means to achieve that ideal state. This paves the way to unleash creativity in the truest sense. It explores what can satisfy an end user or make their lives better and then works backwards in trying to deliver that experience. The core to design thinking is empathy that signifies a deep understanding of human needs and behavior. In informal terms, it is nothing more than putting ourselves into other's shoes.

Applying empathy in a business context helps businesses to understand end users better. Businesses are able to:

➤ Analyze the demands and expectations of users and align products or services that cater to their needs

➤ Discern the existing behavior of the user and influence them to behave in a desired manner

In the context of an enterprise, it is extremely essential to empathize with the employees of the organization. Empathy can play a crucial role in solving complex problems. Within an organization, people come from diverse cultures, backgrounds, abilities, and face unique challenges in their routine jobs. Empathy can help in understanding the challenges faced by diverse groups and their existing behavior, and in turn aid in designing systems that can spur their creativity and engage them better.

Design thinking approach

A typical problem-solving approach would address the following:

➤ What is the problem at hand?

➤ Who are the stakeholders or users?

➤ What are the stakeholder or user expectations?

➤ What are the possible solutions to address the problem?

➤ What is the best solution out of the varied alternates?

➤ How should I go about implementing the solution?

➤ How do I measure the success of an implementation?

While design thinking would also attempt to solve the problem addressing those questions, it would implode the power of divergent thinking by following human-centered approach to problem solving. In most cases, the problems that are being solved by design thinking are wicked problems that do not have a well-defined problem statement and readily tangible solutions.

This is where divergent thinking comes into the foreground. Divergent thinking offers varied perspectives to the problem at hand, gathered from diverse sources. By sourcing innumerable ideas, the prime focus is that of quantity. When people are asked to pour in ideas that won't be judged early, their perspectives widen by spreading the wings of their creative stimuli out of the box. They are more open, transparent, and confident in sharing their ideas, guaranteeing maximum participation. This also introduces the possibility to refine the basic ideas by creating multiple branches from those basic ideas through collaboration. Once the ideas are piled up, convergent thinking is applied to pick the one of the best qualities.

Make a note

Read more about divergent thinking and convergent thinking at `http://www.thinkbrownstone.com/blog/2011/10/26/divergent-thinking-vs-convergent-thinking/`.

Characterizing a design think tank

Design thinking is more of a sociological approach that leverages collective intelligence rather than relying on individual genius. There are certain characteristics that you can observe in people who are good at design thinking, and some of them are as follows:

➤ One who empathizes

➤ Good storytellers

➤ Great observers

➤ Fine listeners

➤ Intrinsically motivated

➤ Widely exposed to multiple disciplines

➤ Creative and adaptive

➤ Forward-thinking and collaborative

➤ Analytical and intuitive

➤ Curious and risk-takers

➤ Perseverant and positive

➤ Thoughtful (intellectual) and thoughtful (considerate)

Why should we apply design thinking to gamification?

In principle, both design thinking and gamification strive to deliver a user-centric experience. We are already cognitive of the fact that gamification is more about engaging the end users by influencing their behavior. This infusion of engagement is rendered effective by applying design thinking principles, such as:

➤ **Understanding the target audience**: Understanding the target audience behavior is an extremely crucial step while devising a gamification system. Design thinking will provide useful insights about the end user behavior and expectations.

➤ **Influencing the target audience**: By carefully observing the behavior of the end user, design thinking can influence the target audience behavior. It would provide valuable insights on the end user motivation and engagement levels. Further, we can discern the causes of disengagement and tailor our strategies accordingly.

➤ **Blending analytics with intuition**: By blending analytics with intuition, design thinking assures that both business objectives and user objectives would be met by the gamification system.

➤ **Broader perspectives**: By facilitating a collaborative environment to gather ideas from diverse sources, design thinking approach can benefit in developing a comprehensive gamification system that incorporates game mechanics, dynamics, and aesthetics to serve all types of users.

➤ **Competencies of a design think tank**: In the previous section, we defined the typical characteristics of a design think tank. This represents the ideal characteristics that would be required for those who design a game-like experience. The ability of designers to empathize, observe, and listen would aid in understanding the user better. By being creative, adaptive, and curious, they can guarantee fun. By being analytical and thoughtful (intellectual), they would stay focused on business objectives. Their ability to tell a story being thoughtful (considerate) would make them include elements that engage the users better.

➤ **Socially wired**: Design thinking encourages community collaboration at every stage and this would help in building a system where the users are socially wired.

> ➤ **Continuous improvements**: By lending a lot of creativity, design thinking strives to improve the output through multiple iterations. Such progressive feedback loops are absolutely essential while designing a gamification system where the user's behavior and engagement levels are analyzed. The insights derived from the analysis aid in continuously refining the system further.

Upholding the rationality of analytical thinking that validates the business objectives, design thinking provides a user-centric approach to gamification ensuring that those business objectives overlap with user objectives.

The design thinking process

A design thinking process is constituted of the following phases:

> ➤ Researching
>
> ➤ Ideating
>
> ➤ Prototyping
>
> ➤ Testing

In its simplest form, this process leads to research on the goals, environment, and user behavior. Further to that, potential solutions are ideated and rated. The solution is then prototyped and tested to gather stakeholder feedback. The output is refined in multiple iterations as a closed loop until there is scope for betterment.

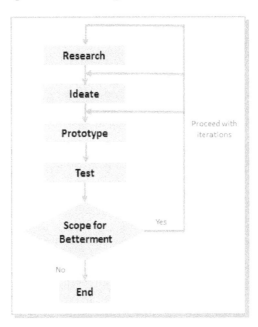

The research phase

Research is one of the most important phases where we understand the goals, environment, target audience, and record the interpretations. There are many a ways in which this research can be carried out to empathize with our end users better. In the context of an enterprise, it is important to understand the culture of an organization. We need a clear understanding of strategic business objectives, problems in the current business context, the employees, and other stakeholders involved.

Research can be further classified into two major categories:

➤ Collecting data

➤ Analyzing data

Collecting data

Collecting data is one of the most fundamental steps while carrying out research. This provides us insights on the enterprise landscape right from policies and procedures to target audience behavior.

Varied data collection techniques include:

➤ **Browsing**: The most straightforward way to carry out research is to browse through the archived documentation about the policies, processes, and guidelines available within the enterprise. Online research would augment this information. This is a preliminary research approach to provide an overview of the dynamics involved. Much of this documentation would already be facilitated as artifacts from the strategy phase.

➤ **Surveys**: The simplest way to carry out research is to survey the stakeholders and end users with a series of questionnaires. When the teams are geographically widespread and there are a large number of respondents, online surveys prove a useful technique to carry out the research activity. This proves effective in scenarios where we need to maintain anonymity.

➤ **Interviews/Meetings**: Interviewing the stakeholders is another technique commonly used to carry out the research. It can be facilitated through face-to-face meetings or telephonic conversations. Either a formal questionnaire approach can be followed as in the case of surveys or the questions can be impromptu by striking a casual conversation. In large organizations, this is feasible only for a sample of the population who could potentially be the pilot users of the system.

➤ **Observations**: This provides an effective way to research the activities carried out by the users. This is the most powerful technique in the context of design thinking as it would provide valuable information about the process, activities, and behavior of the end user. Through observation, the following information can be inferred with much precision:

➢ What activities are involved in the process?

➢ Who are the stakeholders involved in the process?

> ➢ How the tasks are carried out?
>
> ➢ Are the activities performed efficiently?
>
> ➢ What is the level of motivation of the user to perform an activity?
>
> ➢ At what stages is slack experienced?
>
> ➢ What could potentially improve the levels of engagement?

Observation is one of the best techniques to research on the grounds of design thinking because a lot is communicated by humans through their body language. Facial expressions, gestures, and manners convey a lot more about a person's behavior than what is explicitly articulated. Professional movie actors use this technique effectively while preparing for a theatrical role. Either they stay in the close quarters of a person whose profession they portray on screen or perform the job of that person for a considerable timeframe to comprehend their behavior better.

Observation can be exercised in many modes:

> ➤ **Active observation**: An active observer is a person who actively performs the job as a participant to understand the nuances of the tasks performed and the attitude exhibited by the employee while performing the task. This can provide the highest levels of empathy as we directly put ourselves in someone else's situation to experience what they go through. For instance, this can be facilitated in the context of using an online system such as timesheet submission to understand the user experience and empathize as to why there is certain level of disengagement in using the system.
>
> I have always wondered about the motivation levels of those call center representatives who perform cold calls to their customer base to generate leads. These calls are intrusive and customers express their frustration especially when they are in the midst of some important activity. Repeatedly inviting such irate responses can prove disastrous to the morale of a junior trainee. In large organizations, active observation of this nature is feasible only for a sample of the population who could potentially be the pilot users of the system.
>
> ➤ **Passive observation:** A passive observer is a person who merely observes or shadows the end user and observes from a distance as to how the job is performed. For instance, while designing a system for a field sales representative, it proves effective if we can accompany the representative to the site and observe their activities for a day. Same holds good for the case of supervising housekeeping services.
>
> ➤ **Mechanical observation**: Any device can be used to record the behavior of an end user. This is an effective technique that is used in the context of training a new entrant in a call center where the interactions between the call center representative and the customer is recorded for better coaching. Audio playback of these conversations can prove useful to understand the behavior of an employee, especially with regards to productivity and attitude. With regards to access compliance, a video surveillance camera near the gateway can detect the behavior of employees tailgating at an access restricted door. Website traffic can be captured by the system to analyze the user engagement patterns.

> ➤ **Role play**: Role play can be used in situations where the user cannot travel to the location to be an active or passive observer but can experience the same through simulation. This definitely helps to empathize more with the end users. The same technique can also be used for prototyping ideas in the initial stages.

Make a note

Caveat: Choose the right time to carry out the observation. Monday mornings or Friday evenings might not be the ideal working days to carry out observation in an enterprise.

Analyzing the data

After capturing the records, it is extremely important to carry out analytics on the data captured to categorize the responses to derive useful insights and arrive at a user persona. Personas are synthesized from data collected through the research. They aid in visualizing the user goals, the way users interact with the system, and what motivates them to react in certain ways. By attaching a human face or a fictitious character to a user persona, it becomes easy to empathize with employee groups and engage them better.

For example, we can take a certain questionnaire activity to analyze and report, such as:

> ➤ How do users in varied locations in the world respond?
>
> The answer to this could be that an employee in a particular location might be more adaptive to social features in a collaboration site considering the culture in their region than compared to an employee from other location. Gamification strategies for engagement should match these cultural and regional attributes.

> ➤ How do males respond in comparison to females?
>
> The answer to this could be that a male employee might prefer a monetary reward compared to a female employee who might be motivated by a virtual reward.

> ➤ How does Gen X respond in comparison to Gen Y?
>
> The answer to this could be that Gen X might not collaborate as much in a virtual community whereas Gen Y would love to participate and share information with peers.

> ➤ How does a senior leader respond in comparison to a junior trainee?
>
> The answer to this could be that a senior leader might not participate in a quest compared to a junior trainee.

By analyzing these patterns, the system can arrive at a user persona and the services can be personalized or contextualized to the persona representing similar audience groups. For instance, while designing a system for the IT desk service, we arrive at the following user persona in order to understand the target user behavior and design the system to increase the engagement levels:

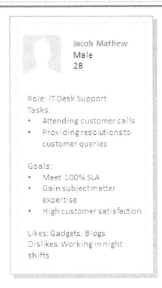

Jacob Mathew
Male
28

Role: IT Desk Support
Tasks:
- Attending customer calls
- Providing resolutions to customer queries

Goals:
- Meet 100% SLA
- Gain subject matter expertise
- High customer satisfaction

Likes: Gadgets, Blogs
Dislikes: Working in night shifts

Apart from the personality traits or roles inferred from user persona, there could be other external factors that can also contribute to disengagement. These patterns should be separated out as outliers and specifically addressed outside the purview of gamification.

A few scenarios could be:

➤ On what days or at what time of the day is more slack experienced by certain groups of employees?

The answer could be that the IT desk support group might experience severe demotivation when they are asked to attend on night shift duties without any perks. This can be inferred from similar user persona as that of Jacob Mathew.

➤ Are there any seasonal or external factors of disengagement witnessed in certain sections of the employees?

The answer could be that employees in a particular location might be severely demotivated by the recession and that could reflect in their disengagement at work.

The ideate phase

Ideate is the core phase where we generate, select, and refine the best ideas that can solve a complex problem or create fresh avenues. Ideation uncovers many a hidden possibilities. Tying to the context of an enterprise, once the research artifacts are available, the ideation is kicked off. This can be broadly categorized to:

➤ Generating ideas
➤ Selecting ideas
➤ Refining ideas

Generating ideas

There are a multitude of techniques available for ideation. Irrespective of the technique that gets implemented, there are certain ground rules to keep in mind while generating ideas:

> ➤ Challenge the status quo

> ➤ Create a wish list

> ➤ Question assumptions

> ➤ Unleash creativity

> ➤ Don't criticize or judge while ideating

> ➤ Collaborate, combine, and multiply ideas

Some common techniques used to generate ideas include:

> ➤ **Brainstorming**: The most popular technique is where employees in a team gather, discuss, and jot down the ideas either with a marker on a whiteboard or use sticky notes on a whiteboard. By focusing on quantity, many ideas get generated and thereby present an opportunity to build upon the basic ideas brought forth by other team members. This works well except when some members of the team dominate too much, debate, and start judging the ideas during the generation process. Especially in organizations that are hierarchy-driven, it is important for those at the helm during brainstorming sessions to empower the team to open up during ideation and share their creative input. It would be good to include a few end users as part of brainstorming session so that they can share wish list as their ideas that will aid in building a system of engagement.

> ➤ **Brainwriting**: This is where employees think and jot down a few ideas on a sheet or sticky note and keep passing it to their peers to read and build on those ideas. Every individual is allowed to write an original idea and also derive inspiration from other's ideas and improve upon it. This stimulates the creative thinking process and also leaves less room for debate and criticism when the thought process is on. This proves very effective in teams where you think certain people are too dominant and suppress other's points of view. This also works when certain people are reticent and would not be open enough to articulate their thoughts but comfortable thinking in isolation before presenting their point of view.

Make a note

Read more about brainwriting at `https://www.innovationmanagement.se/imtool-articles/brainwriting-a-more-perfect-brainstorm/`.

> ➤ **Mind mapping**: Mind mapping can be used as a powerful technique to multiply ideas in varied dimensions. This proves useful in the context of gamification as there could be infinite possibilities that can influence the behavior of an end user. In a mind map, the ideas start from a central node and branch out into varied categories. While this idea generation technique is no different from brainstorming,

organizing the ideas through a visual representation as they are generated allows the employees to expand on varied possibilities around a problem or opportunity. This can be facilitated as a group exercise and there are online tools to depict and share these maps with a larger crowd soliciting their feedback.

➤ **SCAMPER**: SCAMPER is another common technique used to generate ideas. It particularly comes in handy in the context of gamification, because this idea generation technique relies on the notion that everything is a modification of something that already exists. In the context of gamification for employee engagement, the following are sample questions that trigger our thought process enabling us to come up with solutions that can alter user behavior for engagement:

> ➤ **S (Substitute)**: *Should I rename the loyalty program as employee engagement program?*

> ➤ **C (Combine)**: *Should I combine the rewards of virtual currencies and badges?*

> ➤ **A (Adapt)**: *What can I adapt from existing loyalty programs in my gamification system?*

> ➤ **M (Magnify)**: *Can I increase the frequency of rewards?*

> ➤ **P (Put to other uses)**: *Can I follow the loyalty models from the retail industry?*

> ➤ **E (Eliminate)**: *Which incentive does not serve the purpose?*

> ➤ **R (Rearrange)**: *Should I stop all monetary rewards?*

➤ **Crowdsourcing**: What works extremely well in large organizations especially to solve complex problems of a generic nature, is to invite ideas from the crowd by letting them know the problem. This lets every individual or groups to think and submit their ideas through an online system. This works extremely well if floated in the form of a challenge or a quest. Within the enterprise context, when ideas are invited from the employees who are the end users themselves, the problem statements can be framed like a wish list. For instance, we can select a business process and ask them the three things they want to change or include in that process. This indirectly provides us the insights on what acts as a source of disengagement or what could potentially engage them. It serves a large extent to leverage the wisdom of the crowd when it comes to sustainability ideas as it creates a sense of awareness and belonging for the employees.

Selecting ideas

Typically, ideas can be selected based on a single authority or it can be a unanimous decision made by a group of executives or it can be made based on the majority view. There are a series of decision-making models available to help you select of best idea. The following are some decision-making models:

➤ **Voting**: Voting is the most commonly used technique for ranking or prioritizing the most useful ideas that are outputted from the idea generation stage, in a fairly quick manner. The ranking can be done by the following people:

> ➤ A group of senior executives at the helm

> ➤ A group of subject matter experts

> ➢ Participants of the idea generation process
>
> ➢ Project team members
>
> ➢ Cross representatives from the previously mentioned groups
>
> ➢ The entire employee community

Go/no-go decisions can be captured face-to-face or through e-mails if it involves smaller groups, or can be captured formally through an online system if a larger crowd is involved. Depending upon the context, it can also be facilitated by maintaining anonymity.

➢ **Quadrant mapping**: Quadrant mapping is a simple technique to plot the ideas in the four quadrants based on the key drivers on the vertical and horizontal axes. The steps are as follows:

1. Identify the two key drivers for vertical and horizontal axes.

2. A quadrant is plotted with each driver as a continuum from low to high extremes at the end of vertical and horizontal axes.

3. Generate ideas.

4. Plot the ideas in each quadrant.

5. Analyze as to which quadrant has the high concentration of both the drivers.

An ideal gamification system is one that produces a high impact on both business goals as well as user behavior. We can choose them as the two key driving forces with a vertical or y axis representing the impact on business goals and a horizontal or x axis representing the impact on user behavior. Depending on the concentration of the ideas in a particular quadrant, a decision can be made.

➤ **Survey or rating templates**: While the intent is similar to that of voting, this goes one step beyond to specify the criteria or parameters based on which of the ideas should be ranked providing a rationale for the selection process. This can be filled in by the group and submitted through an online system or via e-mail. Based on the stack ranking or the survey responses, the most popular ones are prioritized. A justification behind the decision can be captured as part of the template. There could be bias based on the individuals who rank when rated on a scale.

➤ **The Delphi method**: Originally developed as a forecasting method, the Delphi method facilitates an anonymous summary of an expert's view and guides us to arrive at a decision with rationale. The experts respond to a series of questionnaires in a few rounds. After each round, a facilitator provides an anonymous summary of the expert's opinions with the rationale for their judgment. Other experts can read these views and refine their perspectives. This is the way a consensus is achieved. Gamification might not usually warrant as much anonymity in sourcing or the prioritization of ideas.

➤ **Force field analysis**: This is a useful decision-making technique in the context of gamification as it allows us to analyze the forces for and against a change and communicates the rationale behind the change. Introducing gamification into an existing traditional system might involve good amount of change management and it is extremely important to analyze the impact on user behavior as there are cases where gamification could prove detrimental. Let's assume that an employee is already intrinsically motivated in performing an activity and we attempt to introduce tangible incentives to perform this activity. Though initial interest could peak, subsequently it might kill the inherent motivation and leave the employee disengaged after the initial rollout of the incentive. Analyzing the forces for and against the changes provides us with good insights on the impact of the change.

Refining ideas

The prioritized or shortlisted ideas have to be refined and drafted in a cohesive manner so that they can be prototyped. Preparing a mind map is one good way of organizing the ideas. The ideas can also be drafted in the form of a user story or they can also be fed into the traditional requirement definition processes where they can be documented in the form of a flow chart or a use case. The process of stitching the ideas together and expanding them provides scope to validate the practical considerations, assumptions, dependencies, and constraints. These ideas are further refined while prototyping.

In this step, the game mechanics and dynamics that would be used by the system are carefully thought through. One design consideration while drafting the use case scenarios is to devise the feedback loops that would engage the user with the system. Two types of feedback loops under consideration are:

➤ Engagement loops

➤ Progression loops

The engagement loops operate at the user level to let the user perform an action, provide them with feedback, and thereby motivate them. This motivation, in turn, provokes the user to perform the next action, and so on, in a closed loop.

On the other hand, progression loops operate at the system level where a strategy is devised to engage the end users as part of structuring the entire package that leads them to the path of mastery. It is important to keep the user in the flow zone while leading them to mastery.

The prototyping phase

Prototypes are used to visualize the ideas better and evolve them further. By building rapid prototypes, direct feedback can be solicited from the end users thus providing a scope for refining the output early in the life cycle. Taking a cue from lean startup principles, it always helps to test the waters by building a **Minimum Viable Product** (**MVP**) as a prototype before the actual implementation. This reduces costs, which would be otherwise expended in building a product that does not satisfy the end user needs.

Make a note

Read more about MVP at `http://en.wikipedia.org/wiki/Minimum_viable_product`.

Developing the prototype

In the context of an enterprise where employees are the end users, developing prototypes can prove effective in validating the effectiveness of solutions or services by performing a reality check. An opportunity is provided for the employees to make their own lives better and they pick and choose what they want and how they want it. The prototype can be outputted in any format depending on the context of where it is gamified:

➤ Sketches (such as a storyboard)

➤ Site mock-ups

➤ Working models

➤ Role play (initial stages)

While, traditionally, these prototypes are built as part of the **Joint Application Design** (**JAD**) sessions, the process can be made more efficient through **Joint Application Modeling** (**JAM**) sessions where the employees of different roles such as managers, system designers, visual designers, user experience (UX) designers, developers, testers, and end users can come together to design and develop prototypes. For instance, in order to implement gamification in a performance management system within an enterprise, executives from varied business units such as HR, IT, Operations, Sales, and Marketing can come together with the designers and developers to build prototypes that model the system of engagement.

The testing process

The final phase can be categorized into two steps:

> ➤ Gathering feedback
> ➤ Finishing or proceeding to iterations

Ideally, the benefits of gamification and its influence on end user behavior can be thoroughly testified only after the pilot implementation. Gathering feedback early in the life cycle through a prototype by helping the user visualize what we are trying to build provides an opportunity to fail fast and learn to make appropriate course corrections before implementation of the entire gamification system.

Gathering feedback

Gathering feedback would help to gauge whether the designed system delivers the goods in terms of engaging the end users. Such early feedback during the prototype stages serves to avoid common pitfalls and validate assumptions. This can be facilitated through meetings or interviews or surveys or as part of the JAD/JAM sessions where the prototype is demonstrated to a select group. Depending on the feedback, the team should be willing to refine the prototypes or revisit the ideas and enhance the output until the desired objectives are met.

Finishing or proceeding to iterations

Based on the feedback, we can decide whether we can proceed with the implementation or we have to proceed with further iterations in refining the prototypes, or in some cases, it might warrant additional research to come up with fresh ideas.

By bolstering the creativity of the employee community to work in a collaborative environment and taking into account the perspectives of end users right from ideation to delivering rapid feedback, design thinking helps you to visualize a gamification system that inspires engagement.

Make a note

Caveat: Although design thinking seems an apt fit in the context of gamification, the efforts might still fail because of the lack of system designers who do not know how to seamlessly integrate the game mechanics into a gamification system. If your organization is lately venturing into gamification, hire or contract a game designer or a gaming consultant and enroll them right from ideation or at least during the prototype stages.

A quick recap

Let's recap the design process:

Phase	Steps	Possible Techniques
Researching	Collecting data	■ Browsing ■ Online surveys ■ Interviews/Meetings ■ Observations ■ Role play
	Analyzing data	■ Manual data analysis ■ Analytics and reporting
Ideating	Generating ideas	■ Brainstorming ■ Brainwriting ■ Mind mapping ■ SCAMPER ■ Crowdsourcing
	Selecting ideas	■ Voting ■ Quadrant mapping ■ Survey or rating templates ■ Delphi method ■ Force field analysis
	Refining ideas	■ Mind mapping ■ Traditional requirement definition methods
Prototyping	Developing the prototype	■ JAD ■ JAM
Testing	Testing the prototype	Informal testing methods
	Gathering feedback	■ Online surveys ■ Interviews/Meetings
	Finishing or proceeding to further iterations	

Case study

Continuing the previous example in *Chapter 3, Enterprise Gamification – Strategize*, in the Strategize phase, *how might we encourage the reuse of assets within the enterprise?*, we validated the business case for deploying gamification to promote reuse. Let's apply design thinking to understand what factors can motivate an employee to share knowledge with their co-workers to primarily improve productivity and help them get on board quicker.

The research phase

The research phase involves collecting and analysing data.

Collecting data

Data collection involves the following possible techniques and one of the techniques is chosen:

Possible Techniques	■ Browsing
	■ Online surveys
	■ Interviews/Meetings
	■ Observations
	■ Role play
Chosen Technique(s)	Online surveys

Survey questionnaire sample

A survey questionnaire sample is shown as follows:

This survey attempts to gauge the employees' awareness and attitude towards asset reuse				
Employee Id:			**Date:**	
Q1.	Do you like to share assets that you have created with your colleagues?			
A.	Yes		No	
Q2.	How often do you publish assets?			
A.	Always	Frequently	Sometimes	Rarely	Never
Q3.	How often do you consume assets?			
A.	Always	Frequently	Sometimes	Rarely	Never
Q4.	Does your organization have a well-defined process for reuse?			
A.	Yes		No	
Q5.	Are you aware of the reuse process, policies and standards?			
A.	Yes		No	
Q6.	What do you think are the current barriers to create and publish?			
A.	Not aware where to publish	Not aware how to publish	Tough to customize and catalog content	Tough to update versions	Mention others (if any)
Q7.	What do you think are the current barriers to consume?			
A.	Not aware of how to search relevant content	Not able to find the right version in right format	Not intimated of content updates	Not able to find owner for clarification	Mention others (if any)

This survey attempts to gauge the employees' awareness and attitude towards asset reuse				
Employee Id:			**Date:**	
Q8.	Identify the top 3 benefits of reuse.			
A.	Increased productivity	Getting on board quicker and training	Reduced efforts	Huge cost savings	Rapid development
	Enhanced quality	Enhanced collaboration	Expert identification	Mention others (if any)	
Q9.	Identify what might additionally motivate you the most to reuse assets.			
A.	Recognition for reuse	Incentives for reuse	Tie to performance criteria	Improve user experience	Mention others (if any)
Q10.	Share your innovative ideas of promoting reuse culture within your organization.			
A.				

If a larger audience is involved, this survey can be floated either in an organizational portal or through third-party online survey tools. If you think that employees might not be motivated enough to participate in the survey, you can consider rewarding the most innovative ideas or the best survey responses.

Analyzing data

Data analysis involves the following possible techniques and one of the techniques is chosen:

Possible techniques	■ Manual data analysis
	■ Analytics and reporting
Chosen technique	Both

Once the survey response is captured, the data is analyzed to gather useful insights.

Partial survey response

Partial survey response is shown as follows:

Q1. Do you like to share assets that you have created with your colleagues?

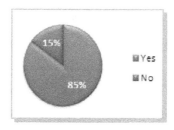

Q2. How often do you publish assets?

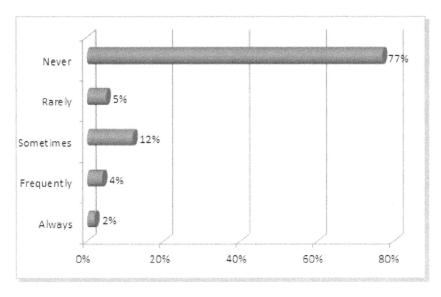

By correlating the responses for questionnaire *Q1* and *Q2* captured in the survey response shown previously, we gather that while 85 percent of them prefer to share data with colleagues, 77 percent never seem to publish those assets to facilitate reuse.

Q9. Identify what might additionally motivate you the most to reuse assets.

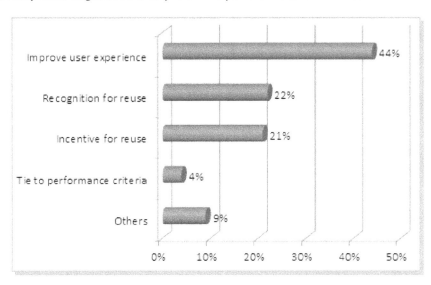

By enhancing social sharing and collaboration, we can see whether the users would engage better. Surprisingly, we also observe from the response to *Q9* that the biggest motivation for reuse seems to be an improved user experience at 44 percent, followed by recognition for reuse at 22 percent, and closely followed by incentives for reuse at 21 percent. It is evident that the system should be designed to include game dynamics that can improve user experience.

The ideating phase

The ideating phase involves generating, selecting and refining ideas.

Generating the ideas

Idea generation involves the following possible techniques and one of the techniques is chosen:

Possible techniques	■ Brainstorming
	■ Brainwriting
	■ Mind mapping
	■ SCAMPER
	■ Crowdsourcing
Chosen technique	■ Crowdsourcing

The ideas are sourced from a crowdsourcing platform where employees log random ideas on what could motivate them to promote reuse culture. The sample ideas are shown as follows:

Selecting the ideas

Idea selection involves the following possible techniques and one of the techniques is chosen:

Possible techniques	■ Voting ■ Quadrant mapping ■ Survey or rating templates ■ The Delphi method ■ Force field analysis
Chosen technique	■ Voting

Against the ideas logged in the platform, employees vote for their favorite ideas. This approach particularly helps as the system can be designed with input from the employees, or in other words, the end users themselves. The sample ideas are shown as follows:

Refining the ideas

Idea refinement involves the following possible techniques and one of the techniques is chosen:

Possible techniques	■ Mind mapping ■ Traditional requirement definition methods
Chosen technique(s)	■ Mind mapping

A group of subject matter experts review the random ideas for their merit, feasibility, and business value. A mind map is created by refining and grouping the best ideas. In this current scenario, the ideation context is depicted at the center and branched out or grouped as three major categories.

A sample mind map is depicted as follows:

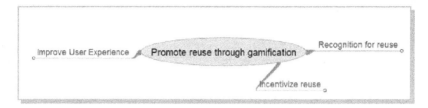

Then each category branches into sublevels of ideas. Here we pick up the first major category, *Improve user experience*, and organize the crowdsourced ideas in many sublevels:

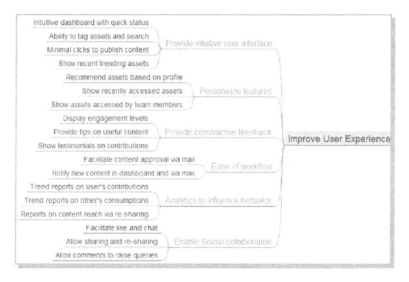

Then we choose the second major category, *Recognition for reuse*, and compartmentalize the ideas logically to two sublevels.

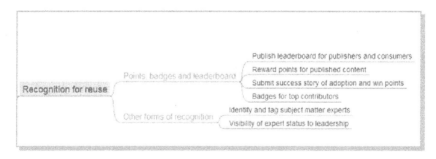

Similarly, we organize the third categorization, *Incentivize reuse*, into two sublevels.

By combining all this together, we obtain a comprehensive mind map where the raw ideas are grouped into a cohesive and comprehensive feature set. The feature set obtained from the mind map can be used *as is*, or converted to user stories and fed as requirements for prototype development, keeping in mind the engagement and progression loops. The formalized requirements and use case scenarios are illustrated in *Chapter 5, Enterprise Gamification – Implementation*, as part of a pilot implementation.

The prototyping phase

The prototyping phase involves development of the prototypes.

Developing the prototype

Prototype development involves the following possible techniques and one of the techniques is chosen -

Possible techniques	■ JAD
	■ JAM
Chosen technique(s)	■ JAM

A JAM session is conducted to develop prototypes in order to validate the feasibility of requirements early in the life cycle. The game elements are incorporated seamlessly into the system to accelerate employee engagement.

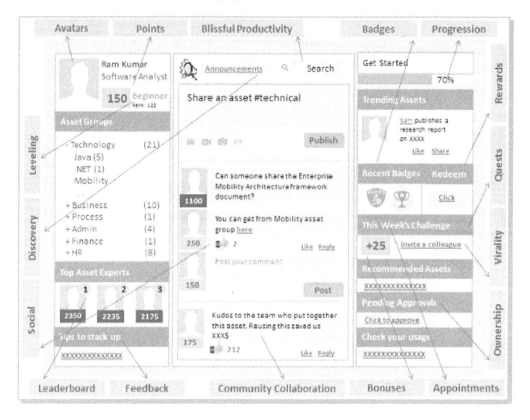

The testing phase

The testing phase primarily involves gathering feedback from the stakeholders.

Gathering feedback

Gathering feedback involves the following possible techniques and one of the techniques is chosen:

Possible techniques	■ Online surveys
	■ Interviews/Meetings
Chosen technique	■ All

Feedback is gathered through all possible means to check whether the goals can be met, and then pain points are addressed. The feedback is used to further enhance the functionalities and improve the overall end user experience.

Finishing or proceeding to further iterations

Depending upon the feedback gathered on the system functionality and user experience, we further iterate or complete the design process and move towards an actual implementation.

Summary

In this chapter, we learned about the design thinking approach and how to apply design thinking to gamification. Conducting research on the background and target audience, ideating on a potential solution, prototyping the solution, and testing the outcomes early in the life cycle by gathering end user feedback is a recommended design workflow to deploy gamification.

In the next chapter, we will learn about the steps involved in implementing a gamification system that engages employees.

> 5

Enterprise Gamification – Implementation

In the previous chapter, we learned how to apply design thinking to gamification. In order to accomplish the business objectives, we collected and analyzed data, generated and shortlisted relevant ideas, built rapid prototypes as the working models, solicited user feedback, and went through multiple iterations to refine the output. This reinforces the confidence to gear up towards actual implementation.

In this chapter, we will cover:

> ➤ How to go about a pilot implementation
> ➤ How to measure and monitor outcomes
> ➤ What the considerations are to keep in mind before scaling from pilot to full-blown implementation

Gearing up for implementation

It is always recommended to kick-start gamification efforts in an enterprise with an incremental approach (pilot implementation) as opposed to big bang adoption (full-blown implementation).

There are varied reasons as to why a pilot implementation for gamification is recommended. Here's a list of a critical few:

> **Gamification involves change management**: Gamification initiatives involve huge change management and there could be some resistance within an enterprise setup towards adoption. For instance, if the organization is typically hierarchy-driven, a social feature introduced by the gamification system might confuse the employees as it might be in direct conflict with their standard communication protocols. In this case, lack of clarity leads to lesser adoption. There could be very many reasons why the user is not embracing the change. Even with extreme due diligence and extensive research efforts carried out prior to implementation, the success of the system still lies with the user's willingness or mindset to adopt the changes. This can be critically examined during a formal pilot execution with minimal investment.

Make a note

Read more about change management here:

`http://en.wikipedia.org/wiki/Change_management`

> **Tough to perfect the design**: We already observed that most gamification systems fail due to inadequate design. Despite applying design thinking and techniques, it is quite tricky and tough to perfect the gamification design in one shot, and only with continuous monitoring of user behavior for a stipulated time period can the user experience be further enhanced.

> **Effectiveness of gamification**: It is very important to understand that gamification augments the existing system to provide business value and cannot replace the existing system. Any gamification initiative can be deemed successful only when the business objectives are accomplished with a significant amount of change in user behavior as desired. There could be varied possibilities while evaluating the effectiveness of gamification in the workplace, for example:

>> An employee could disengage with the system because of inherent issues in the system and even after deploying gamification, there could be no improvements

>> An employee could already be engaging with the system at a certain level without deploying gamification and a poorly implemented gamification system might disengage the employee

>> An employee could engage with the system for reasons other than gamification

> ➢ An employee could crack the gamification system and might manipulate the system for the incentives and it could prove detrimental to the overall objectives

> ➢ The effectiveness of gamification can be put through rigorous testing during a pilot and the strategy can be reevaluated for its merit or tailored in a better fashion before being adopted in the big bang style.

➤ **Establishing quantitative return on investment (ROI)**: It is never straightforward to establish ROI from initiatives that involve gamification, as the engagement metrics could provide intangible benefits that in turn drive the primary outcome or indirectly help achieve the business goals. It is essential to monitor the impact of gamification initiatives on key performance metrics and their efficiency to drive towards the accomplishment of end objectives before continuing to invest on a large scale. This way we can also invite top-level executives to experience the benefits of the pilot system and obtain executive buy-in for further investments.

➤ **Analytics is the key**: The key aspect of a gamification system is its ability to generate huge volumes of data insights on the user behavior. When the employee spends time with the system of engagement, they leave a lot of footprints, which in turn could be fed into the system in a closed loop for continuous improvements. A pilot study provides an immense opportunity to make the system more robust.

Selecting the right gamification platform

A critical step to perform before pilot implementation is to evaluate and select the right gamification platform and the associated tools.

Build versus buy

A decision should be made whether to invest and build the gamification platform ground up in-house or to leverage the host of existing platforms available on the market.

While each platform needs to be evaluated on a case-by-case basis for its suitability in an enterprise context, some of the key considerations in selecting an appropriate platform would include, but not be limited, to the following:

➤ Rich feature set (game mechanics)

➤ Integration (web/mobile)

➤ Programming (API)

➤ Rule configuration

➤ Rule administration

➤ Toolkits (widgets)

➤ Performance and security

➤ Scalability and availability

- Data persistence
- Analytics and reporting
- Pricing model
- Vendor credentials

Although this necessitates careful evaluation of each of the parameters we just listed, at the outset, if the range of features is available out of the box, the existing platforms available in the market can be leveraged. If a lot of customization is required and the organization is equipped with in-house skills to build and maintain a solution, then it is better to build a custom platform as a service.

Defining a roadmap for pilot implementation

A pilot implementation roadmap typically covers the following aspects:

- **Business context**: The first step is to define the business context, the business need, or the problem statement addressed by the pilot implementation.

- **Pilot description and goals**: The next step is to define the description of the pilot project and the goals to be accomplished. The goals can be further decomposed into specific milestones based on geography, employee types, and employee roles depending on the context of implementation.

- **Scope of implementation**: The scope of pilot implementation is a detailed clarification of what is in scope, and what is out of scope.

- **Solution**: The solution is elaborated in detail to show how it will help achieve the business goals by addressing the problem statement, covering the following aspects:
    - Feature set/functionalities
    - Business rules (game mechanics)
    - Proposed technical architecture
    - Key benefits

- **Stakeholders**: The stakeholders and their respective roles are to be clearly defined. RACI matrix is one of the tools that can be used for this purpose to define and track the roles and responsibilities of the stakeholders involved.

Make a note

Read more about the RACI matrix for stakeholder management here:

http://en.wikipedia.org/wiki/RACI_matrix

➢ **Support artifacts**: A bunch of support artifacts need to be collated from the organizational repository and strategy-cum-design phases to aid the pilot implementation.

> ➢ **Existing business processes**: Documentation of existing business processes comes in handy when establishing an additional workflow to accommodate game elements. For instance, currently the approvals could go through multiple screen navigations, and post the implementation of a gamification system, the approval could happen with a single click from an e-mail notification or through a mobile app.

> ➢ **Infrastructure, hardware, software requirements**: The infrastructure, hardware, and software requirements are identified and listed.

> ➢ **Target audience**: The target audience is one of the key aspects to consider while designing and implementing a gamification system. In *Chapter 3, Enterprise Gamification – Strategize,* we saw various means in which the target audience can be classified. In *Chapter 4, Enterprise Gamification – Design,* we learned how to research this information before designing our prototypes. Taking these as input for the pilot implementation, the target audience types need to be clearly categorized and their needs or expectations have to be elaborated.

> ➢ **Documenting target behavior**: Ideally, the target behavior should promote the business objectives. Only if employees spend time on the platform, they would be engaged to perform certain activities that might have a direct or indirect impact on the business outcomes. Also the engagement has to be sustained in a continuous fashion such that the user feels the time invested is worthwhile and feels the need to revisit. The expected target behavior covering these aspects needs to be documented and tied to the Key Performance Indicators.

> ➢ **Feedback loops**: Both the engagement and progression feedback loops have to be interleaved in the gamification system to ensure higher degrees of engagement for all types of users. We already discussed in brief about the engagement and progression feedback loops in *Chapter 4, Enterprise Gamification – Design,* as part of the *refining ideas* section in the design thinking process.

> ➢ **Prototypes**: In *Chapter 4, Enterprise Gamification – Design,* we learned how to design and develop prototypes. These prototypes constitute valuable archetypes also referred to as **Minimum Viable Product** (**MVP**) and prove extremely valuable before proceeding with implementation.

Make a note

Read more about MVP here:

`http://en.wikipedia.org/wiki/Minimum_viable_product`

➤ **Integration requirements**: The existing system needs to be integrated with the gamification platform (in-house or third-party) and there could be other dependent systems as well from where the data flows in. All the integration points need to be highlighted and the requirements are to be elaborated in detail.

➤ **Performance and security considerations**: Any system would have performance and security considerations within an enterprise and these details are to be elaborated.

➤ **Dependencies, assumptions, constraints, and risks**: Any dependencies on internal systems and processes, any assumptions made prior to implementation, specific constraints within the organization posing challenges for change management like executive management support, and the risks involved in the implementation are to be clearly documented.

➤ **Defining resources**: We further define the team size and the ideal mix of resources required to execute the pilot.

➤ A typical resource mix includes:

  ➢ Visual designers

  ➢ User experience design experts

  ➢ Developers

  ➢ Testers

  ➢ Leads/managers

➤ Preferably, game designers with prior design experience in video games can be extremely handy in providing valuable inputs on incorporating the right game elements in the non-game context for increasing user engagement.

➤ **Defining schedule milestones**: The detailed implementation schedule along with the schedule milestones is finalized and published.

➤ **Evaluate pilot implementation outcomes**: Defining the success criteria for the pilot is a crucial step as the go/no-go decision for a large scale implementation depends on the successful outcome of the pilot phase. By and large, gamification leverages the psychological aspects to influence employee behavior and provides qualitative benefits as compared to quantitative benefits. However, the following steps are carried out in an attempt to quantify the success:

  ➢ **Define KPIs and metrics**: This is a critical step where the key performance indices and the formula to measure them are identified and listed. This also includes additional metrics and measures that can testify engagement.

  ➢ **Baseline metrics**: For the sample size under consideration for the pilot, baseline metrics so that they can prove useful while comparing the delta improvements that gamification brings to the system post implementation.

  ➢ **Record findings**: The pilot findings are formally recorded and archived in the organizational lessons learned repository.

> ➤ **Evaluate pilot success**: This clarifies how the pilot success criteria would be evaluated. The metrics from the baseline version (pre-implementation) are to be compared to the post-implementation metrics to gauge the improvement levels provided both operate under similar conditions.

➤ **Obtaining approvals and sign-off**: Necessary approvals and sign-off are obtained from respective stakeholders for the pilot implementation plan.

Building the system

Let's discuss a sample implementation to understand the key aspects covered in the pilot implementation roadmap.

Case study

Continuing the previous example in *Chapter 3, Enterprise Gamification – Strategize,* in the **Strategize** phase, *How might we encourage reuse of assets within the enterprise?*, we already validated the business case for deploying gamification to promote reuse. We applied design thinking and categorized the relevant ideas in a mind map and proceeded to develop, test, and refine the prototypes. This case study highlights the implementation details covering critical functionalities and a few sample use case scenarios.

Business context

The asset management process within the enterprise needs to be looked at again. There are too many disintegrated portals where the assets are currently maintained for varied contexts and there is no integrated view of the assets. There is no mechanism to validate the assets. The engagement level is poor with respect to the consumption and adoption of best practices, thereby employees end up reinventing the wheel. Employees exhibit slackness in publishing or updating these assets so that it is available for reuse by their colleagues. Owing to poor user experience in the existing systems, there is lack of ownership and motivation. Employee productivity has hit an all time low in the last quarter. With the increase in organizational size, it takes significantly more time to onboard new entrants.

Pilot description and goals

The pilot project aims to launch a new platform that provides an integrated view of the assets. The project also aims to add social and gamification elements in order to increase user engagement in creating, publishing, and consuming assets promoting better reuse. The pilot rollout targets the following goals:

➤ Increased productivity (20 percent)

➤ Quicker onboarding and training (shorter by 2 days)

➤ Enhanced collaboration

➤ Expert identification

➤ Defect reduction

Feature set

The key features of the system include:

> ➤ Publish assets
>
> ➤ Consume assets
>
> ➤ Gamification rules (game mechanics and dynamics)
>
> ➤ Collaboration features
>
> ➤ Analytics and reporting

Technical considerations

The asset management system would be integrated with the custom gamification platform comprising of the following:

> ➤ Admin workbench to configure the business rules and user profiles
>
> ➤ API calls (typically REST/JavaScript) to send the activity stream and also retrieve the user specific data
>
> ➤ Widgets to be embedded in the site
>
> ➤ Analytics and reporting dashboards to measure the engagement levels

Target audience and behavior

For the asset management system, the targeted pilot users are the employees in an IT organization. The users can be classified based on the activities they perform in the system as follows:

> ➤ Publishers
>
> ➤ Consumers
>
> ➤ Approvers
>
> ➤ Moderators

While all the users can function as publishers and consumers, only select users have the privilege to act as approvers and moderators. The target user behavior is tied to the goals that we want to accomplish. A sample illustration is as follows:

Objective	Publisher	Consumer	Approver	Moderator
Increased productivity	■ Minimal clicks to be published on the site ■ Publish content from the explorer view in the local system ■ Pre-populated meta data	■ Instant click for consume on the site ■ Consume content from the explorer view in the local system ■ Advanced search options	■ E-mail notifications for approval ■ Approval enabled through mobile app	■ Automated reporting dashboard ■ Real-time analytics and notifications
Quicker onboarding	■ Getting started virtual tour			
	■ Upgrade assets ■ Asset groups notifying recently published content	■ Recommendations based on recent trends ■ Recommendations based on profiles ■ Tips when searching assets	■ Approval checklist	
Enhanced collaboration	■ Like, share, re-share, comment on content			
	■ Integration with communication channels like e-mail, chat			
Expert identification	■ Badges for expert levels based on overall contribution			
	■ Experts listing specific to asset groups			

The game mechanics are tied around the target audience behavior. For example, since it is inferred that users might value the disk space they earn to store or share assets in an enterprise context, they are awarded free storage space to sustain continuous engagement.

Make a note

Refer to *BR1* in *Gamification rules (game mechanics)* section for more details, later in this chapter.

Devising feedback loops

The engagement and progression feedback loops are devised in order to drive engagement and enable them to reach the path of mastery, respectively.

Engagement loops are facilitated by providing feedback to the user to perform certain actions. For instance, users are encouraged to complete the startup activities by splitting the task into multiple steps and indicating the progress.

The progression is achieved by letting the users travel a journey from beginners up to the expert level:

> ➤ Beginner
> ➤ Intermediate
> ➤ Specialist
> ➤ Expert

Experts are given special power and access to sustain their engagement levels.

 Make a note
Refer to *BR5* in the next section for more details.

Gamification rules (game mechanics)

Typically, **business rules** (**BR**) are configured in the administration workbench of the gamification platform's rule engine. The rules are triggered based on the activities performed by a user.

BR1: Space incentives for activities performed

Activity	Free space
First-time login	25 GB
Complete six of the startup activities as a quest within a stipulated period	50 GB
Take a virtual tour of the system	5 GB
Skill profile completion	10 GB
Set a local folder to upload and download assets	2 GB
Invite a colleague on-board	2 GB
Choose redeem option for reuse credits	1 GB
Download mobile app	10 GB
Every 25th asset published	100 GB
Every asset that has more than 1000 downloads by unique users	100 GB

BR2: Reuse credits (points) for activities performed

Activity	Reuse credits
First asset published	100
1 asset published	50
1 asset upgraded	50

Activity	Reuse credits
1 asset downloaded by a unique user	5
1 best rated expert response	50
1 testimonial for business value	100
25 assets in a particular category	250
Hitting every 10000 reuse credits	1000

BR3a: Badges for continuous engagement

Badge name	Qualifying reuse credits for badges
Beginner	Less than or equal to 1000
Intermediate	More than 1000
Specialist	More than 5000
Expert	More than 10000

BR3b: Badges for specific quests

Badges	Sample quests
Advocate	Submit the top 10 assets you consumed this year
Master mind	Submit how your asset generated business value for the community
Ethic guru	View code and ethics assets and complete the quiz
Mad scientist	Submit a best practice tool
Virus	Submit idea to spread an asset viral

BR4: Leaderboard for publishing the rankings of those who engage or contribute the most.

➤ All the reuse credits or the points earned qualify for leaderboard

➤ The points are added up to publish the rankings

➤ Leaderboard stack ranked against the following community:

  ➢ Global employees

  ➢ Employees in the geographical country of the user

  ➢ Employees in the geographical region of the user

  ➢ Department of the user

  ➢ Role of the user

  ➢ Team members of the user

- Option to filter based on the previously mentioned categories
- Option to filter based on overall and relative leaderboard
- An engagement score for the user on a scale of 10 while clicking on each of the asset groups
- Top experts listing in each of the asset groups

BR5: Rewards/value for reuse credits

Every 1,000 reuse credits would translate into one of the options that can be chosen by the user:

- $50 worth book credited to organizational library
- $50 donated for underprivileged children's education
- $50 worth redeemable gift coupon

The credits can be accumulated up to any level. Once redeemed, it would be debited from the account. For every 10,000 reuse credits accumulated, 1,000 credits would be bestowed as dividends.

Once 10,000 reuse credits are reached, the users would be offered the expert badge and added to the 10,000 + club and given special and exclusive access privileges that include the following options:

- Eligible as moderators to the system
- Eligible for annual awards program
- Sponsored with special access to external conferences and symposiums
- Sponsored for mentoring programs from world-class institutions
- 25 percent discounts on certifications

Make a note

This reward structure is elaborated further in *Chapter 6, Sustaining Outcomes and the Road Ahead.*

Sample use cases

The sample use cases for the gamification system are as follows.

Use case 1: Getting started

Overview

This use case describes the workflow of the asset management system for a first time user to get started with the system. It highlights the gamification elements included in the system to drive engagement.

Actors

➤ Pilot users

➤ System

Pre-condition

The pilot user is configured for access to the system and receives a mail notification with the username and password details.

Main flow of events

1. The user logs in to the asset management portal by entering their username and password.

2. The user is awarded free space as a first-time user (refer to *BR1*).

3. It displays the *Get started* page with the message that free space is available for the user in the workspace.

4. It displays the series of steps to complete six of the startup activities (refer to *BR1*).

    1. Step 1: Take a virtual tour of the system.

    2. Step 2: Complete skill profile details.

    3. Step 3: Set up a local folder to upload and download assets.

    4. Step 4: Invite a colleague on-board.

    5. Step 5: Choose the redeem option for reuse credits (refer to BR5).

    6. Step 6: Download mobile app.

5. The user is allowed to either proceed with the next step or skip the steps.

6. The user is thrown the upload option to upload and publish an asset or skip.

7. The user is shown the asset management dashboard.

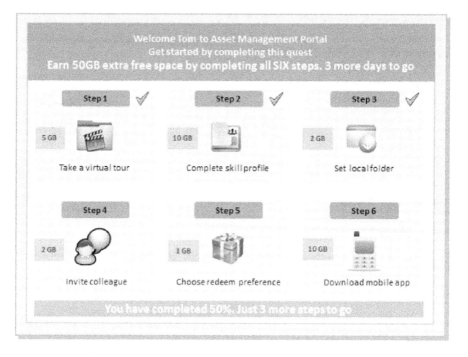

Use case 2: View home page

Overview

This use case describes the workflow of the asset management system for an existing user while viewing the home page. It highlights the gamification elements included in the system to drive engagement.

Actors

> Pilot users
> System

Pre-condition

The existing user has logged in to the asset management system with their credentials.

Main flow of events

1. The home page is displayed

2. The user is shown the following sections and features:
   > Basic profile details
   > Reuse credits (refer to BR2)
   > Recent badges (refer to BR3a, BR3b)

- ➢ Current ranking in leaderboard (refer to BR4)
- ➢ Upcoming challenges or quests
- ➢ Tips to climb up the leaderboard
- ➢ Search options:
  - ➢ Basic (any text)
  - ➢ Advanced with the following criteria to choose from: Topic, Owner, Tag, Department, Asset type, Team
- ➢ Progress percentage of getting started, indicating a proportion of the steps left for the user to complete the onboarding process
- ➢ List of asset categories or groups that the user is subscribed to by default
- ➢ List of asset categories that the user visits often
- ➢ Notifies the count of the assets that the user has not visited against asset group listing
- ➢ Lists the following additional features:
  - ➢ Recently uploaded assets in the community and the conversations around it
  - ➢ Link to create and publish assets
  - ➢ View, like, share, comment options
  - ➢ E-mail/chat options
  - ➢ Subscribe to colleagues and follow their assets
  - ➢ Recently trending assets in the global community
  - ➢ Recently accessed assets by the team
  - ➢ Recommended assets based on skill and interests defined in the profile
  - ➢ Help tips to consume the right assets while searching randomly
  - ➢ Testimonials on top contributions
  - ➢ Dashboard link to view analytics reports and leaderboard widgets
  - ➢ Pending approvals (based on user access privileges)

3. User clicks on one of the functionalities and proceeds

Use case 3: Publish assets

Overview

This use case describes the workflow of the asset management system for an existing user to publish assets. It highlights the gamification elements included in the system to drive engagement.

Actors

> ➤ Pilot users
> ➤ System

Pre-condition

The existing user has logged in to the asset management system with their credentials.

Main flow of events

1. The user logins to asset management portal with username and password.
2. The user clicks on one of the asset groups.
3. The user is shown an engagement score (refer to *BR4*).
4. The user is shown the experts in the particular asset group.
5. The user is notified about the count of the assets that the user has not visited against each asset group.
6. The user clicks on *Attach File* and the file dialog opens (branch out to alternate flow of events) in order to publish an asset.
7. The user chooses the document from the system and uploads the file.
8. The user is thrown options to populate more details on the asset and tag it.
9. The user clicks on *Publish*.
10. The user receives a mail notification that the asset has been submitted for approval.
11. The approver receives a mail notification that a new asset is pending approval.
12. The approver opens the document from the explorer view and reviews the document.
13. The approver right clicks and approves the document.
14. The user receives a mail notification that the asset has been published.
15. The user receives reuse credits (refer to *BR2*).

Alternate flow of events

1. The user accesses the asset management folder from the explorer view.

2. The basic tagging details for the asset are pre-populated.

3. The user clicks on *Publish* (back to *main flow of events* at step *11*).

Use case 4: Upgrading a consumed asset

Overview

This use case describes the workflow of the asset management system for an existing user to consume and upgrade assets. It highlights the gamification elements induced in the system to drive engagement.

Actors

➤ Pilot users

➤ System

Pre-condition

The existing user has logged in to the asset management system with their credentials.

Main flow of events

1. The user clicks on one of the asset groups and chooses the asset they want to upgrade.

2. The user clicks on *Upgrade Asset.*

3. The user is given the option to upload the upgraded asset.

4. If different from the primary author, the user is credited as secondary author to the asset.

5. The primary author and approver receive a mail notification that a new asset has been published.

6. The primary author and approver review the document from the explorer view.

7. The primary author and approver right click and approves the document.

8. The system notifies the subscribers of the group about the upgraded asset.

Use case 5: Analytics and reporting

Overview

This use case describes the workflow of the asset management system for an existing user to view the analytics dashboard. It highlights the engagement metrics.

Actors

➤ Pilot users

➤ System

Pre-condition

The existing user has logged in to the asset management system with their credentials.

Main flow of events

1. The user clicks on the view analytics and reporting dashboard.

2. The user is displayed the following gamification widgets (periodic views):

   ➢ Number of assets published, consumed, and shared, and the asset groups the user has subscribed to

   ➢ Badges that the user has accumulated so far

   ➢ Experts listing for each asset groups

   ➢ Leaderboard stack ranked against the following communities:

      ➢ Global employees

      ➢ Employees in the geographical country of the user

      ➢ Employees in the geographical region of the user

      ➢ Department of the user

      ➢ Role of the user

> ➢ Team members of the user

> ➢ Option to filter based on the previously mentioned categories

> ➢ Option to filter based on overall and relative leaderboard

3. Trend reports on user's contributions (periodic views).

4. Trend reports on other's consumptions on user's published assets (periodic views).

5. Trend reports on top contributors of assets month on month

> ➢ Top publishers

> ➢ Top consumers

> ➢ Top influencers (based on sharing and re-sharing)

> ➢ A sample leaderboard is depicted below.

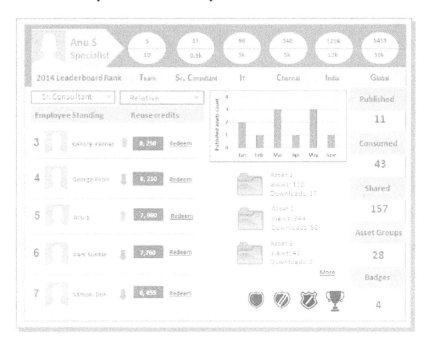

Measuring and monitoring outcomes

Organizations define and measure **Key Performance Indicators** (**KPI**) that constitute the primarily targeted business objectives and other metrics to evaluate the success of the pilot implementation. With respect to KPIs, the baseline version is captured before pilot implementation and compared with the data captured after pilot implementation. The other metrics and measures that are specific to pilot implementation indirectly influence the KPIs and also provide a good overview on the user engagement levels and its impact on the KPIs. Once measured, all of the data is translated in the form of actionable insights or reports, as well as analyzed and monitored for further inference on the outcomes.

Case study

Continuing the case study implementation, the Key Performance Indicators and other metrics are captured to gauge the promotion of asset reuse.

Defining Key Performance Indicators (KPIs) and metrics

The Key Performance Indicators and metrics are defined as follows:

KPI/other metrics	Formula
Productivity (KPI)	Size/effort
On-boarding time (KPI)	Number of days between joining date and project allocation date
Defect density (KPI)	Number of defects/size
Effort variance (KPI)	(Actual effort – planned effort)/planned effort
Schedule variance (KPI)	(Actual end date – planned end date)/ (planned end date – planned start date)
Subscription rate	Total number of registered users/total number of pilot users
Asset publish efficiency	Total number of users who have published at least one asset/total number of pilot users
Asset consumption efficiency	Total number of users who have consumed at least one asset/total number of pilot users
Asset publish rate (periodic)	Number of assets published by user/total number of assets published
Asset consumption rate (periodic)	Number of assets consumed by user/total number of assets consumed
Progression rate	Average number of days for a user to move from one level to another level of expertise
Mastery rate	Number of experts in the system/total number of pilot users
Asset reach	Number of likes and comments and shares on an asset/number of users who visited the asset

The other measures (periodic and life-time engagement) are as follows:

> ➤ Relative rank of user with respect to other users in an asset grouping
> ➤ Number of user views for an asset

- Number of downloads for an asset
- Number of likes for an asset
- Number of comments for an asset
- Number of shares for an asset
- Number of subscribers for an asset group
- Number of upgrades on an asset
- Total count of assets published in a period
- Total count of assets upgraded in a period

Measure KPIs and metrics

The Key Performance Indicators and metrics data are captured by the system and the reports are analyzed to evaluate the success of the pilot implementation.

Evaluating pilot success

The baseline metrics captured prior to pilot implementation are compared with the metrics post implementation and the engagement levels are gauged. The Key Performance Indicators are compared against the goals set. If the goals are met and the targeted delta improvements are achieved while comparing the pre and post implementation outcome, the pilot is deemed a success. The learning is documented and used to correct the deviations during the full-blown launch. If the pilot is unsuccessful, a retrospection meeting is called, involving all the stakeholders in deciding on the next course of action.

Some of the questions to ponder:

- Was the pilot roadmap followed?
- Did the selected platform prove effective?
- What are the major roadblocks encountered?
- Were there any integration challenges?
- Was the pilot able to demonstrate significant improvement in the KPIs?
- Did the additional metrics and measures signify more engagement?
- Are there any gaps observed based on which the original solution needs to be revisited?
- Overall, did the pilot achieve the business objectives?
- Is the learning documented in the form of recommendations?
- What is the next course of action?

Scaling from pilot to full-blown launch

Assuming that the pilot implementation is successful, the implementation can be rolled out to all users across the enterprise or the intended audience.

Some of the key activities to be watchful of include:

> ➤ Gaining approval from key stakeholders after evaluating the pilot success

> ➤ Drafting the full-blown implementation roadmap

> ➤ Identifying and documenting the additional requirements or modifications for full-blown implementation

> ➤ Feeding back the recommendations from the pilot phase

> ➤ Validating whether the assumptions made in the pilot phase still hold good

> ➤ Anticipating potential scale-up issues and being prepared with mitigation steps

> ➤ Being ready with the infrastructure requirements and environment required for full-blown implementation and doing the capacity planning

> ➤ Staging the rollout, addressing customization requirements of each segment, and identifying champions to scale the program

Make a note

The comprehensive steps from a process standpoint to plan and execute a full-blown launch are kept out of the scope of this book as they do not differ much with respect to the implementation of gamified versus non-gamified systems.

Summary

In this chapter, we learned how to start off the implementation journey from pilot launch, record the pilot findings, and if deemed a success, scale to full-blown implementation.

In the next chapter, we will learn about sustaining the outcomes, deploy a few useful adoption strategies, and contemplate what's lying ahead for the future of enterprise gamification both in the short and long term.

➤ 6

Sustaining Outcomes and the Road Ahead

In the previous chapter, we saw a pilot implementation and the means to measure and monitor the outcomes. It is important to sustain those outcomes in the longer run.

In this chapter, we will cover:

➤ How to sustain outcomes

➤ How to develop adoption strategies

➤ What is in store for the future of enterprise gamification

Sustaining outcomes

Rewards and recognition programs commonly prevail at workplace to motivate the workforce. No wonder rewards have become a straightforward means to sustain end user engagement in a gamification system.

While rewards can be broadly classified as tangibles and intangibles, a good gamification system should excite the user by providing a value that is perceived as most important to them.

Any incentive that is provided to the employee can be broadly grouped into four categories:

> **Status**: Status refers to relative position of oneself with respect to others. A generic example could be the soldiers or sportsmen winning the badge of honor for their achievements. In the gamification context, badges and the leaderboard typically constitute the status that the employees can exhibit proudly. Status lends itself very close to gamification since it instills a sense of pride amidst the community and accelerates engagement.

> **Access**: Access provides the users with an exclusive opportunity to something that is viewed as a privilege. An example of exclusive access in a workplace could be an invite for lunch with the leadership team. Access can be a choice of reward during occasions of special achievements such as crossing a milestone or a mastery level.

> **Power**: Power is exercising control over others. In a website, the administrators typically have more power as they can enroll and provide access to other users. While power is a great source of motivation, it cannot be entitled at all situations as it might be governed by stringent polices expressing confidentiality or security concerns in an enterprise setup. Power can also be considered as a reward choice for special achievements.

> **Stuff**: "Stuff" typically implies tangibles representing money, goods, or sometimes intangibles such as virtual rewards. It is not an ideal or the preferred candidate for rewards in a gamification context especially concerning the sustenance of outcomes in the workplace. Stuff is perhaps a good means to drive the employee to get started but gradually, the system should kindle an intrinsic desire to participate or contribute.

> Some of the cases where stuff could prove effective are at the following junctures:

>> The initial stage to kick start the momentum

>> The intermediate levels where a critical milestone is achieved

>> Instituted as a periodic honor (such as annual top contributors)

>> Announce stuff upfront to drive more participation

>> Significant efforts are invested towards performing an activity

A few more examples for each scenario include:

> - An employee is motivated if he or she stands a chance to succeed among his peers (*Status*)

> - An employee is motivated if he or she gains an exclusive access to premium service such as sponsorship to attend a technical conference (*Access*)

> - An employee is motivated if he or she is privileged enough to control colleagues such as moderating a community (*Power*)

> - An employee is motivated if he or she is provided some monetary reward considering the stellar effort invested (*Stuff*)

Make a note

Caveat: While stuff cannot be ignored altogether, too much of stuff might dilute the initiative as it could either kill the intrinsic motivation that is already present to perform an activity or the user could manipulate the system in order to pocket the stuff. It would serve as a best practice to identify and substitute actual stuff with status, access, and power in the appropriate mix in order to sustain the outcomes.

Developing adoption strategies

We have already seen how gamification is a change management initiative that doesn't have a predefined formula for successful user adoption. While a good design and clear definition of reward structure is critical to basic adoption, a specific strategy needs to be in place to drive employee engagement within an enterprise.

The typical steps include:

1. Promoting awareness
2. Helping with tips
3. Starting with incentives
4. Spotting moderators and evangelists
5. Publishing success stories

Promoting awareness

Any initiative needs good amount of marketing and propaganda in the first place to attract the right amount of attention from all parties involved. Targeted marketing campaigns can be launched to promote the initiative internally within the organization.

Helping with tips

The employees should be able to seamlessly jumpstart with the system once rolled out. Step-by-step tips or illustrations on getting started would help to get the community on board at least once. From there on, the success rate would depend on system's design and relevance to target audience.

Starting with incentives

It would be a good idea to start with stuff or tangible rewards. That would again serve the purpose of getting the community on board, beyond which the intrinsic drivers can sustain the momentum. The steps to get started can be incentivized.

Spotting owners and evangelists

It is extremely critical to choose the right owners/moderators/administrators to the system who have the onus to facilitate and offer adequate support. It is also essential to spot the right evangelists or ambassadors who have the zeal to adopt early, try out the features of the system, and spread the good word to the rest of the community. It is also a good idea to incentivize or provide special privileges to the early adopters who are extremely critical to the success of the initiative. For instance, if an evangelist invites a colleague to try out the system, he can be incentivized.

Publishing success stories

Both the owners and the evangelists should be encouraged to publish and reiterate success stories. More importantly, the benefits have to be clearly elucidated to the community. Clear articulation of how the business goals are accomplished supported by associated metrics and statistics to prove the positive outcome can generate huge interest in the community.

Beyond Points, Badges, and Leaderboard

Albeit not a thumb rule, all gamification systems have become synonymous with **Points, Badges and Leaderboard (PBL)**. PBL is an integral component of gamification and is definitely a nice ingredient to include in the recipe, but it is not a complete meal to guarantee sustenance by itself. Earning points or badges or topping the leaderboard might become a ritual if they are not attached to concrete end outcomes that the user can relate to.

While the basic strategy would be to accumulate points for redeeming tangibles, the employee might lose interest in due course of time to engage in the activity if the tangible isn't attractive. The badges are a sense of pride, no doubt but again, accumulating the similar badges repeatedly in the kitty is not going to engage the user in the longer run as it does not signify further leveling.

Leaderboard also fails to engage the users in the longer run for varied reasons, such as:

> A leaderboard that is not time bound fails to engage the user continuously

> A leaderboard that does not attempt to drive any purpose except to stack the rankings

> A leaderboard that does not provide any relative view with the employee's team

> An employee is already on top and has no motivation further

> An employee is ranked too low that he or she loses interest to compete

A good gamification system should think beyond PBL to drive better adoption on a continuous basis. When deploying gamification to influence the user behavior, the system itself cannot comprise of elements that renders it boring and stale.

Apart from PBL, there are quite a lot of intrinsic rewards that the employees value in the enterprise setup. They can be broadly classified as follows:

Motivation catalyst	Examples
Sense of surprise	Creating unanticipated moments
	Adding the fun factor
Sense of progression	Reinforcing progressive feedback
	Enhancing skills
Sense of recognition	Visibility at workplace
	Appreciation from colleagues in social graphs
Sense of value	Empowerment to embark on certain activities
	Identifying substitutes
	Contributing to a larger purpose

Sense of surprise

This is achieved by creating the unanticipated *wow* moments or including the *fun* elements.

Creating unanticipated moments

We have heard about the *aha!* moments in the context of innovation. Akin to that, unanticipated moments in the context of gamification pay off really well to engage end users. Employees should be surprised with rewards or announcements at unexpected instances. In anticipation of such moments, they develop a sense of continuous engagement.

Adding the fun factor

Wherever possible, introduce elements in the system that makes it more fun and interesting. This in itself would sound like a reward that keeps the user glued. Establishing social graphs and discovering like minds can bring in some element of fun and interest in the workplace.

Sense of progression

This is accomplished by nurturing and reinforcing growth.

Reinforcing progressive feedback

A good way to sustain employee interest in the context of gamification is to provide him or her with regular feedback and reinforce their progress. The analytics module of the gamification system should prove effective in continuously providing personalized feedback to the employee at every level of interaction. Be it the steps left for them to get started, tips to win more points, awarding badges and topping the leaderboard, recommendations that suits their profile, interest levels and needs, acknowledgements from their social graphs, recent activities that are trending, upcoming quests, and so on, transparent feedback is a great way to influence the end user behavior.

Enhancing skills

Leveling up the employees in terms of skills and abilities is one of the best intrinsic rewards that will amplify the engagement levels. Incentivizing the milestones while reaching certain levels and publicizing the mastery attained is a great way to sustain engagement.

Sense of recognition

This is bestowed by accrediting and evangelizing contributions.

Visibility at workplace

Gaining good visibility at workplace and being recognized by the leadership team or experts in the community is one of the biggest motivating factors for employees in an enterprise who might otherwise not get the right opportunities to prove their mettle. A transparent gamification system can bring talented employees to limelight when they indulge in certain activities that are of great value to the organization. For example, in the context of asset management reuse discussed in the earlier chapters, a business consultant can claim top honors from leadership team for sharing a unique business model that has helped many a groups in winning larger client deals.

Appreciation from colleagues in social graphs

Earning repute for themselves among the peers serves as one of the best motivators in an organizational setup for employees. The gamification system provides ample opportunity for employees to share their knowledge, showcase their expertise and skills, and gain appreciation from their close circles. For example, in the context of asset management reuse discussed in the earlier chapters, an employee could create an asset that has generated the maximum number of likes and comments. This would trigger the employee to further engage with the community and contribute.

Sense of value

This originates with empowerment and expands with empathy.

Empowerment to embark on certain activities

The gamification system should allow the employee to embark on certain activities in the system and provide them with a sense of empowerment. For example, in the context of the asset management reuse example discussed in the earlier chapters, once 10,000 reuse credits are reached, the users are offered the expert badge and added to 10,000 + club and given special and exclusive access privileges such as sponsorship for an exclusive program or discount on certifications. As they have reached the highest level of expertise, they might lack further motivation to participate. This kind of empowerment ensures that the users who have actively contributed are engaged on a continuous basis.

Identifying substitutes

Instead of awarding points or goods, certain substitutes can be awarded as incentives based on the context. For example, in the context of asset management reuse discussed in the earlier chapters, instead of awarding points, free space (GB) is awarded for the first-time login or for bringing a new user onboard. The employee can perceive real value out of such substitutes rather than mere tangibles or virtual goods.

Contributing to a larger purpose

An employee would be intrinsically motivated to participate in an activity if they enroll into the objectives or the larger purpose. For example, in the context of asset management reuse discussed in the earlier chapters, there is a value associated with attaining certain amount of reuse credits that the employee can identify as every 1,000 reuse credits produces a monetary value that is likely to be spent towards a good cause like a book credited to organizational library or money donated for underprivileged children's education.

Rewards approach

An ideal approach to rewards at work place can be derived from Maslow's hierarchy of needs. Maslow outlined a hierarchy of needs whereby humans are motivated to reach the highest level called self-actualization signifying the state in which a human realizes their optimal potential and remains intrinsically motivated. The levels are usually represented in the form of a pyramid with self-actualization being at the top of the pyramid. Maslow also urged that unless we satisfy the lower levels, we cannot expect one to move up to the top.

Make a note

Read more about Maslow's hierarchy of needs at `http://en.wikipedia.org/wiki/Maslow's_hierarchy_of_needs`.

We can draw parallels to Maslow's hierarchy levels in the context of employee needs within an enterprise as follows:

Pyramid levels	Employee needs	Examples
5	Physiological needs	Salary components
4	Safety needs	Work place safety and health benefits
3	Social	Working relationship with supervisors and peers
2	Esteem	Recognition and growth
1	Self-actualization	Learning and development
		Meaningful and challenging tasks
		Engagement at work

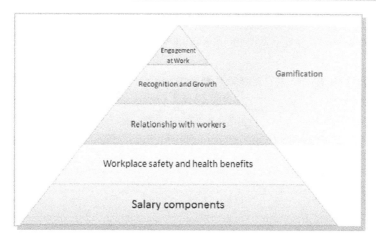

While the fifth and fourth levels are quintessential aspects for motivation that are more of prerequisites, the top three levels can be supplemented by gamification initiatives. A good gamification system should be able to push the employee gradually to a self-actualized state, maintain them in the flow zone and sustain their morale. This is where the employee realizes and performs to their fullest potential. This is where the employees are focused, collaborative, resourceful, and compassionate. This is when the employees exhibit the highest degree of engagement by being outcome-oriented.

Reward structure

There are no right or wrong ways to reward. Be it tangible or intangible, there are different instances in which the rewards can be offered. This has to be customized according to the context of gamification. The tabulation below could be one way of generalizing the reward events, reward types, and game elements to influence user behavior:

Reward events	Reward types	Game elements
First time user	Status, Stuff	Points, Badges, Leaderboard, and Tangible/Virtual goods
Starting an activity	Status	Points, Badges, and Leaderboard
Completing an activity	Status	Points, Badges, and Leaderboard
Completing an activity successfully / Performing best	Status and Stuff	Points, Badges, Leaderboard, and Tangible/Virtual goods
Bring another user on board	Status	Points
Every nth time an activity is performed	Status	Points and Leaderboard
Every n duration an activity is performed	Status	Points and Leaderboard
Completing levels / Accomplishing specific milestones	Status, Access, Power, and Stuff	Points, Badges, Leaderboard, Tangible/ Virtual goods, and beyond PBL
For attaining highest or prestigious levels	Status, Access, and Power	Beyond PBL
Perform a simple task	Status	Points
Perform a unique task	Status and Stuff	Points, Badges, Leaderboard, and Tangible/Virtual goods
Perform a stipulated cum significant task	Status and Stuff	Points, Badges, Leaderboard, and Tangible/Virtual goods

Reward events	Reward types	Game elements
Perform an unanticipated task (thrown as a surprise)	Status and Stuff	Points, Badges, Leaderboard, and Tangible/Virtual goods
Accumulate certain number of points	Status, Access, and Power	Badges and beyond PBL
Participate in a challenge or a quest	Status	Points and Badges
Win a challenge or a quest	Status	Points and Badges
Annual/Periodic top contributions	Status, Access, Power, and Stuff	Points, Badges, Leaderboard, Tangible/Virtual goods, and beyond PBL
For gathering n acknowledgements from other users	Status	Points

Seeding the culture

If you are in search of one factor that can definitely guarantee employee engagement, it has to be the feel good factor. All of us love to feel good about ourselves, don't we?

Let me list down some of the things that makes us feel good at the workplace:

> When someone greets and smiles at us
> When someone compliments us for our acts
> When someone acknowledges our good work
> When someone entrusts us with challenging tasks
> When someone thinks that we are the right person for the job
> When someone tries their best to retain us in their team
> When someone recognizes our distinct or special skills
> When someone goes out of the way to assist us
> When someone values our contributions
> When someone decides something in our favor

Apart from the competitive salary component and incentives, positive working relationships, striking a good work-life balance, and earning the trust of supervisors and peers are some of the basic employee expectations that create a healthy work environment.

Going by the 80–20 rule, 80 percent of the positive engagement is attributed to 20 percent of the feel good factors. This feel good factor has to be deep-rooted in the culture of an organization.

If the organization can help the employees feel recognized for their good work, enable them to pursue their passion, guide them with career growth opportunities aligned to their passion, and encourage them to volunteer for a good cause, the employees would develop a sense of belonging in the organization.

Self-esteem at work, enhanced productivity levels, and improved quality of life can foster engagement. Though the expectations of each employee would be different, these feel good factors can act as effective change agents in achieving an engaged culture at workplace that can better employee satisfaction and reduce employee turnover.

Gamification initiatives have to be targeted at identifying and accelerating those feel good factors that should prevail in the culture without which the initiatives will prove futile. At the end of it, gamification is not about points accumulated or the goods won; it is more about influencing the employees to exhibit a positive and reinforcing behavior in the workplace. And it doesn't work in silos. As the gamification system continues to increase the engagement level and notify the behavioral patterns through the analytics dashboard, the stakeholders at varied levels in the enterprise need to pick up the cues and help the co-workers.

Each employee has to own the system and effectively use the different game mechanics and dynamics towards creating better outcomes. It is equally important for every stakeholder in the organization right from executive leadership, middle management, and ground level employees, to seed the culture of transparency, goodwill, and collaboration in the workplace in working towards a common goal.

As we saw in *Chapter 1, Employee Engagement and Gamification*, millennials get motivated by nurturing interpersonal relationships at workplace crossing the barriers of hierarchy and gamification could prove an ideal choice to facilitate such social interactions. This, in turn, helps to establish healthy working relationships. No doubt gamification represents the system of engagement at workplace but the employees, especially those at the senior levels, need to create a culture of engagement that percolates down under.

The road ahead

I find this as the most interesting section to pen down. Predicting the future of enterprise gamification is interesting because none of us actually know what's in store but can unleash our imagination to foretell the future keeping in view the current landscape. Let's analyze what the various possibilities could be in the near- and long-term.

Near-term possibilities

We'll take a closer look at the near-term possibilities in the following sections.

Gamification aliases

As evident throughout the course of the book, gamification is not a new invention. It is definitely something that we have been practicing in some form or the other, be it in the business world or otherwise. Perhaps the term, the structure, and a formalized process on how to go about it are new to us. Considering that the reward and the loyalty programs of the past have evolved as gamification keeping the end user experience in mind, it could pave way to another interesting term in the future.

People have already started rechristening gamification as "pointification" or "engagification". Let me join the bandwagon to coin few new terms like "behaviorification", "UXificiation", "influencification", or "humanification" —pun intended. However we term it, the direction is definitely to move beyond the points, badges, and leaderboard to create an optimal, personalized, and engaging experience for the end user. In a workplace, the employer and employee should come together and work towards a common goal, be it to provide high quality service to the customer or ensuring that their organization gains a competitive advantage in the industry. Ideally, gamification should present a win-win-win situation for the employers, employees, and the customers.

Make a note

Read more about pointification at `http://www.vvolume.com/?p=344/`.

Gamifying core business processes

In *Chapter 2, Gamification in Action,* we learned about the scope and the applicability of gamifying business processes within an enterprise setup. In the near future, more and more core business processes could be brought into the gamut of gamification to engage the employees at workplace. There could be many challenges along the way, such as the systems could be sturdy with heavy dependencies on other enterprise-cum-third-party systems and driven by complex business rules offering less flexibility for redesign. There could be regulatory, compliance, and legal considerations obliging it to be rendered more serious than fun and engaging. There could be access control issues. Despite these issues, enterprises would continue to introduce gamification constructs to core business processes to improve employee productivity and end user efficiency.

More social, more collaborative

Social business is the new norm and the hierarchical models in the organization structure are becoming flatter. Employees are more open, transparent, and seek to collaborate with each other. Gamification lends itself naturally to provide those social connections and facilitate those interactions. Employees feel more engaged when they are allowed to share knowledge, exchange ideas, and win their peers' acknowledgement. They are willing to learn from each other, build on each other's ideas, and operate in a collaborative environment where everyone has a place for themselves rather than always vying for a position by beating others.

This collaborative spirit would be amplified in the near future by the employers to leverage the wisdom of the crowd to create disruptive innovations by engaging the employees better. The power of collective intelligence is humongous in producing business value of the highest order and gamification could prove extremely effective in unleashing this huge potential. Great innovations would no longer be confined to the corridors of executive offices but would happen on the ground. Organizations have already started and would continue to leverage this potential.

Making it mobile

In view of IT consumerization, smartphones have become an integral part of our lives and the employees from all industries are craving to use them as a work companion. The benefits of mobility are huge in terms of real-time access to data anywhere, anytime, enabling faster decisions and actions. The extended data access, inherent features such as the camera, video, GPS, accelerometer, gyroscope and access to zillions of utility-cum-social apps from the corporate context to personal use, enterprise mobility magnifies employee productivity. With organizations promoting **Bring Your Own Device (BYOD)** and **Bring Your Own Apps (BYOA)** policies, gamified experiences offered via the smartphone can deliver real value to the employees and engage them continuously. Be it delivering notification for one-click approvals or conveying real-time feedback or necessitating rapid action or providing guidance for pitching sales to customers, the possibilities are infinite in the near future.

Tapping Big Data

Huge volumes of data are the golden eggs laid by the gamification systems, which are not just a system of engagement, but also a system that can facilitate business intelligence insights. The employees of an organization leave huge trails of data while engaging with the gamified system. These digital footprints can help understand the employee profiles better and personalize the user experience. This data can also provide additional insights on the employee behavior at varied instances, the employee's attitude towards the organization, including their team, supervisors, colleagues and at times, customers too. These insights should be in turn used to influence the behavior of the employee towards productive means. Organizations have started realizing this huge potential and continue to enhance the analytics and reporting modules in the gamification system and feed those insights back into the system for continuous, real-time monitoring and facilitating corrective actions.

Make a note

Read more about big data at http://www.theguardian.com/news/2013/nov/22/rapid-development-in-big-data-analytics-has-led-to-increased-investment.

More failures anticipated

As we speak of the potential, it is also important to realize that more and more gamification efforts may continue to fail in near future due to the reasons highlighted in *Chapter 3, Enterprise Gamification: Strategize*. Enterprises should put together a cross-skilled team of professionals who can deeply understand the culture of the organization and the varied systems, processes, and stakeholders involved and approach gamification by applying design thinking while keeping the end user experience in mind. It is not going to be easy to perfect this and more and more gamification efforts would prove futile either due to lack of relevance, lack of poor design, or lack of understanding on how to tie the business objectives to the user behavior.

Organizations would take sides on gamification with some doubting its credibility. But as long as the hype surrounds it, they would be attracted to it and willing to test the waters. When it comes to deploying gamification for employee engagement, some of the questions that would continue to do the rounds include:

> ➤ Is it the right strategy?
> ➤ Is it worthwhile to experiment?
> ➤ Is it worth the efforts?
> ➤ Is it worth the investment?
> ➤ Are there significant returns?
> ➤ How can I get it right?

Although there is no single formula to predict the outcome or guarantee the success, there will be a group of players who would continue to experiment, strategize, invest time, and cost with vigor to get it right. Some may fail and quit. Some may fail and learn. Some may succeed and sustain. The hype would definitely stay on for few more years. If approached smartly, the hype would be justified with fruitful outcomes.

Long-term possibilities

We'll take a closer look at the long-term possibilities in the following sections.

Goodbye to the term "gamification"

The term gamification might vanish altogether. This prediction is primarily because of the fact that in the future, a design thinking and human-centered approach to design might be the norm while designing any system and the game elements would be automatically injected as part of the process rather than explicitly being called out for. The factors that are essential to engage the end user would seamlessly integrate in the core systems rather than be applied as a cosmetic layer on top to merely showcase the points or ranks.

Engaging with wearable gadgets

We have already observed that gamification and wearable technology have started to partner in the context of the personal wellbeing of the employees. With more devices like smart watches and smart glasses hitting the market, the next big phenomenon within an enterprise could be **Wear Your Own Devices (WYOD)** and **Wear Your Own Apps (WYOA)** that makes it all the more engaging for the employee. The gamification system should leverage these wearable items as the user interface. Not just that, this could also open new gateways to push behavioral data back to the system as a form of closed feedback thereby providing more useful insights to continuously monitor and accelerate the engagement levels.

Instead of delivering an online course on compliance illustrating the do's and don'ts in a facility, an employee can wear the glasses and walk around the facility. As they adhere to right practices, they can be congratulated with a message or points flashing on the glasses and as they violate a policy, they can be given some feedback on the right practice. This data can be captured in the backend system to award credits. This could make a compliance course extremely engaging.

Field sales representatives could be equipped with essentials on the glasses or watch when they set out to meet the customers to close out deals. Face recognition can help to mine the customer profile and personalized tips can be delivered on the wearable. This can instill confidence in the sales representatives to strike a meaningful conversation with the customer and aid them in their acquisition pursuits. With new technologies such as touchscreen t-shirt displays and wearable TV all set to hit the market in few years, wearable items can take the gamification world by storm by allowing employees to set goals and receive instant feedback. The possibilities are endless.

Exploiting big data

Many organizations have started tapping into the potential of big data in the context of gamification. In future, the fullest potential of big data could be exploited. When it comes to understanding an employee, apart from the data available in the backend system that carries the basic profile details of an employee, the social profile data can be meshed for additional insights. The real-time conversations that the employee generates in the enterprise collaboration systems can prove extremely valuable.

For instance, if the organization is planning to launch a social networking platform, more options to template the unstructured data should be designed in the system such as grouping or tagging the conversations. This in turn can enable the system to capture the user persona at a detailed level than merely sticking to basic information such as age or the gender of the employee. Business intelligence should be built into the systems to mine this data and gather useful patterns about the employee. On continuous interactions, the system should be trained to respond to these patterns in creating a personal connection with the user.

Imagine the capability of big data and analytics to predict and plot a set of employees in an organization in a heat map and auto-detecting the employees who move out of the flow zone. The outliers signifying those employees who experience anxiety or boredom can be plotted in the map, categorized into groups, and strategies can be formulated to pull them back into the flow zone.

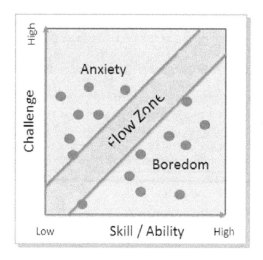

Learning from adjacent worlds

If gamification is all about motivating, engaging, and influencing the end user behavior, can lessons be learned from the adjacent worlds apart from the world of virtual games? One example could be the world of sports.

Lesson #1: Competing with equals

Competition is quite common in the sports arena. In an individual sport, if two players who are ranked in the top ten compete against each other, they train harder. They strive to deliver a superior performance. The tournament organizers and the spectators benefit the most as a great match could be on the cards. At the same time, the competition actually helps each individual to uplift their standards where both of them could surpass their personal bests. On the flip side, if the two players are not of equal caliber, there is a possibility that the stronger opponent might become complacent and the weaker opponent might feel too anxious to compete.

Correlation: Instead of stack ranking the employees against each other in a leaderboard, imagine that the system is trained to spin the game elements differently.

➤ Can the system create a spirit of competition among equals (employees performing similar roles or with similar levels of experience) by pushing them to tread the path of mastery by surpassing their own standards taking inspiration from their colleagues?

➤ Can the system detect signs of complacency or anxiety amongst employees and notify the appropriate stakeholders?

➤ Can the system offer tips to overcome signs of frustration or anxiety?

Lesson #2: Engaging a coach

A coach plays a very critical role in the life of a sports person. They are the greatest motivators, influencers who shape and guide the players to perform at their best. The training offered by the coaches to the players is systematic, scientific, time-tested yet personalized and performance-oriented. They instill the belief that one can win over others and themselves. They teach the players on handling both success and failures. They constantly communicate with the players and provide real-time and critical feedback on the player's progress. They stay focused on the objectives and also have a solid understanding of the individual players and their attitude. They adapt their teaching methodologies to suit an individual's potential and style of play. They continuously innovate and seek ways to improve the player's skills.

Correlation: Imagine a gamification system that can play the role of a coach for every employee. In this case, the employer can delegate the job of a coach or mentor to the system and the employees would want to stay close and get engaged with the system.

➤ Can the system train the employees knowing his or her potential, interest, and areas of work?

➤ Can the system come up with personalized recommendations that drive the employee's performance?

➤ Can the system continuously monitor their progress and provide real-time feedback?

Lesson #3: Building team synergy

Team sports are where players work towards accomplishing a shared goal. The feeling of representing their country could give them all the more pride. Team members set goals, communicate with each other, manage conflicts, support each other in testing times, and strive to reach their targets. Though significant individual contributions are valued and recognized, the players are more focused on the team's win rather than individual glory. The players are picked based on their potential and style of play but offered strategic roles where they can optimally perform considering the overall team composition. The players learn to adapt, acquire social interaction skills, and value the importance of teamwork in such a setup.

Correlation: Imagine a gamification system that can leverage the power of teamwork to accomplish great things in the organizational setup.

➤ Can the system identify and bring together a group of employees to accomplish common objectives?

➤ Can the system facilitate collaboration amongst a diverse set of employees who are geographically spread?

➤ Can the system aid the employees to innovate in a distributed group?

➤ Can the system identify and manage conflicts?

This is just a fictional correlation from the world of sports. Likewise, there could be many other worlds adjacent to the game world with similar characteristics, from where there could be multiple takeaways in order to design the system that has the potential to engage the workforce.

Changing personas

Rather than modeled user persona types, the system could treat every single user as an individual persona knowing their traits at a granular level in future. That brings us to the debate on system persona. So far, we have only been discussing the user persona where the system can understand the varied users based on their persona. Should the systems be also designed with a persona where they can wear different hats and react differently based on the situation? The system should be able to dynamically switch persona and interact with the user. Imagine that we have a virtual assistant in the system to engage the user; the assistant should become a male persona automatically if a male employee logs in rather than asking the employee to choose it.

Relating to a purpose

Humans are always focused on the end outcomes that they can relate to. Typically employer fixes a goal and expects the employees to accomplish that goal. After fixing the goal, employer lists down the series of activities to be performed. Instead, if the employer knows the purpose that it will serve for the employees or meaningful outcomes that hold value to the employees, they can create a bridge between their goals and the employee goals to drive the engagement. Then the series of activities that the employee has to perform to accomplish those goals can be easily identified for better engagement.

A story scenario

Quoting a personal story, I didn't engage as much to do research involving my domain at my workplace. I was introduced to Flipboard and somehow it excited me to flip articles into a web magazine that sounded more like professional bookmarking to archive great articles for future reference. I tied the research activity to flipping wherein I started reading the articles and simultaneously flipped them. While the former activity sounded mundane, the latter activity pushed me to perform the former activity in an engaged fashion. Likewise, reading non-fiction or serious printed material doesn't engage me as much. When I am asked to undertake such an activity, I tie it to an activity of my interest, which is blogging as the end outcome. I do the former activity of reading because the end outcome is to blog about it. Many a times, don't we undertake an activity that is tied to charity or sustainability?

In future, if the gamification system is built with intelligent analytics to spot such meaningful end outcomes for the user, won't that sound like the system manipulating a human? Of course with good intent!

Think and act human

Gamification systems would reinvent themselves with changing times. The most important or fascinating aspect about games is their unpredictability. Although the rules remain constant, every time the user is challenged with different permutations and combinations making it all the more engaging. The outcome is equally unpredictable. If the game elements become mundane and predictable, the engagement will naturally dip.

The humans, players, or employee with whom the system interacts is also of an unpredictable nature. Humans are not just associated with skills but they are also associated with emotions. As of today, gamification systems place a great deal of emphasis on the skills/abilities of the player or challenges faced by the players but ignore the emotional aspects of the player. Under all similar conditions, a skilled employee might not react the same way at this moment in time as compared to a different moment in time. A sentiment analysis engine can analyze a text pattern to detect the sentiments expressed by the users in the conversations. That brings us to the question of whether a human expresses their real feelings through text alone.

More often, it is not just about what you say but it is also about how you say it. There are many modes in which humans communicate apart from text—through voice intonation and body language—and these constitute the full spectrum of human emotions. Newer form of analytics such as emotional analytics is evolving in the field of communications. There are already niche solutions on the market that claim that they can detect the mood of the user and respond accordingly.

We have observed a number of advancements in the field of artificial intelligence, robotics, and natural user interfaces that have pushed the horizons of human-machine interactions. A number of disruptive innovations such as driverless cars and the commercial drones have started performing tasks that were once confined to the boundaries of the human race. That brings us to the next question for the future—can the system be wired to think like a human? If yes, the gamification systems of future can take the place of a human companion that understands a human completely. It can respond to user's physical and emotional needs, detect a user's attitude, influence a user's behavior, and coach, coax, and engage the user to perform at optimum levels. Game on.

Summary

In this concluding chapter, we learned how to sustain outcomes by providing a value to the user that is perceived as most important by them. We learned a few strategies that could aid users to adopt the system better. We also explored the future of enterprise gamification, envisioning a wide variety of forthcoming possibilities, both in the context of near- and long-term.

Let's do a quick round-up of what we covered in the book:

> ➤ We started off by understanding the need for employee engagement and how gamification could potentially help in accelerating the engagement levels

> ➤ We went on to appreciate how gamification can be put in action within enterprise business processes and achieve the business objectives

> ➤ Then we took a strategic approach to gamification and validated the business case for its applicability by coalescing the business objectives and the user objectives

> ➤ We saw how design thinking processes could be effectively applied towards designing a gamification system

> ➤ We illustrated how to start small with a pilot implementation, learn from the pilot findings, and scale further

> ➤ We explored the means to sustain the outcomes, examined a few strategies to drive further adoption, and wrapped it up with a sneak preview of the future

I hope that this book helps you to understand the concept of gamification in depth so that you can validate whether it can be applied as a strategy to solve the problem at hand and drive meaningful outcomes instead of sandwiching it. I also hope that the illustrations aid you with an actionable approach towards strategizing, designing, and implementing an enterprise gamification system that results in amplifying the employee engagement levels and be able to sustain the outcomes in the longer run. Then there is this final hope that you found this book, rather the journey, useful and engaging.

www.ingramcontent.com/pod-product-compliance
Lightning Source LLC
LaVergne TN
LVHW081345050326
832903LV00024B/1322